Chinchillas

Chinchillas

A Guide to Caring for Your Chinchilla

By Donna Anastasi
Photographs by Ellen Bellini

Laguna Hills, California

Karla Austin, *Director of Operations and Product Development*
Nick Clemente, *Special Consultant*
Barbara Kimmel, *Editor in Chief*
Marylou Zarbock, *Consulting Editor*
Amy Stirnkorb, *Designer*
Indexed by Melody Englund

The chinchillas in this book are referred to as *she* and *he* in alternating chapters unless their sexes are apparent from the activity discussed.

Library of Congress Cataloging-in-Publication Data

Anastasi, Donna.
Chinchillas : a guide to caring for your chinchilla / by Donna Anastasi ; photographs by Ellen Bellini.
p. cm. — (Complete care made easy)
Includes bibliographical references and index.
ISBN 978-1-933958-15-6
1. Chinchillas as pets. I. Bellini, Ellen. II. Title.

SF459.C48A53 2007
636.935'93—dc22

2007016508

BowTie Press®
A Division of BowTie, Inc.
23172 Plaza Pointe Drive, Ste. 230
Laguna Hills, California 92653

Printed and bound in Singapore
11 10 09 08 1 2 3 4 5 6 7 8 9 10

Acknowledgments

I WOULD LIKE TO ACKNOWLEDGE KECIA SANTERRE of Furry Flowers, who has kept exotics for over two decades and lives in the midst of her herd of seventy-plus chinchillas. Kecia graciously opened her "chinchillary" to show and tell all about these unique animals. This book came to be through countless hours spent "talking chins" with me, sharing her experience. Many of the animals pictures within are from Furry Flowers Chinchillas. For his review of Chapter 8, I am indebted to William Sager, DVM, of Sager Animal Hospital, who has been practicing small animal and exotic veterinary medicine for twenty years. I am grateful for Libby Hanna's many and varied contributions and for my husband Tom and everything he did. And finally, I want to thank Lawrence and Kera from whom I learned firsthand the ways of the chinchilla.

—Donna Anastasi

MANY THANKS TO KECIA SANTERRE, Judi and Emily Poirier, Libby and Stephen Hanna, and Haley and Tom Wendell for allowing me to photograph them and their beautiful chinchillas. Thanks to Dr. Douglas Meade, Valerie Baier, Olivia Sowell, Amanda Crespo, Valentin Tenev, Allison Bergeron, Tricia Chapman, Amy Anastasi, and Katie Anastasi for being wonderful models. Thanks to Andy, Dimitra, Laurie, and Julie for help with chinchilla wrangling. Special thanks to Amy's chinchillas, Lawrence and Shikera, who endured many hours of photo shoots without so much as a nip. Thank you to Donna Anastasi for writing another great book and allowing me to be a part of it. To my wonderful husband, Jon: thanks for your help and participation. It made it that much more fun.

—Ellen Bellini

Contents

CHAPTER

1

What Is a Chinchilla?

This inquisitive chinchilla has the night vision and superb hearing characteristic of her species.

CHINCHILLAS ARE INQUISITIVE, SENSITIVE, INTELLIGENT, ACTIVE animals. They make playful and affectionate companions to the privileged few in their lives whom they come to love and trust. If you long for such a companion but are prone to allergies, there's great news for you: despite sporting the thickest coat on earth, chinchillas are hypoallergenic! This means that while you may be allergic to other fuzzy companions, you may find that you can keep chinchillas without a problem. These small animals are relatively easy to care for, but they must be cared for properly, as they have very specific diet, housing, and environmental needs. They are becoming increasingly common as pets, despite being somewhat exotic looking and difficult to describe. The Chinese word for *chinchilla* proves the point: it means "dragon cat"!

What is it? A rabbit? A squirrel? Sporting big ears and tiny front paws, dense fur, and a curled-up tail, the chinchilla keeps people guessing.

Storyteller Libby Hanna explains the origin of the chinchilla—seemingly part bunny, part squirrel—in the following fanciful way:

> In the beginning, the Creator called out to all the creature spirits to come before him, where he would give them form. One by one, each animal spirit, from the leopard and the eagle to the tiniest field mouse, came before him; and he parceled out wings, feet, fins, and fangs, such as each would need to go forth and prosper. All day, animal spirits came without a form or shape and left as the animals we know today.

But the shy chinchilla kept her distance, afraid. Finally, as the day drew to an end, the Creator called for any other animal spirits out there to come now, for this was their last chance. Only then could the gentle chinchilla summon up her courage and approach him. He told her she was the very last one, and he was almost out of parts.

Peering into the boxes about him, he found a pair of dark bush baby eyes and great big bat ears. As he shuffled boxes, he shook his head. There didn't seem to be a set of matching legs left: only one pair of little tiny front paws and great long back legs with just three toes and a funny odd one stuck halfway up the side. They would have to do. After dumping out the contents of the last boxes, he found a curled squirrely tail and long whiskers, ones made for a much bigger animal. He placed all the spare parts on the chinchilla, and she took form before him. He tilted his head and squinted at the strange-looking creature. The animal's large eyes looked wet, as though she were trying not to cry.

Studying his work, he thought for moment. Then, an idea came to him. He reached up, and taking one of the soft gray hairs off his own head, he placed it on the chinchilla's back. Instantly grew the thickest, softest, warmest, most beautiful coat in all the earth. With a shy, grateful smile, she leaped and bounded away, up to a crevice on a rock on a high mountaintop almost touching the heavens, where the chinchilla lives to this very day.

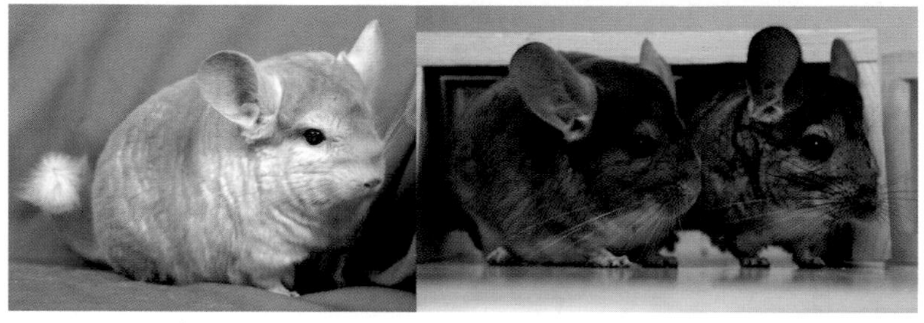

There are three chinchilla body types: (from left to right) the blocky *brevicaudata*, the lean *lanigera*, and the slight *costina*.

Scientific Classification

Scientists' attempts to explain the chinchilla are a bit more, well, scientific. They classify these mammals as belonging to the order Rodentia and the suborder Hystricognathi (which includes guinea pigs but not other pet rodents such as mice, rats, gerbils, or hamsters), the family Chinchillidae, and the genus *Chinchilla*. There are two main species of Chinchilla: *brevicaudata* and *lanigera*. Of the two, the *lanigera*, or long-tailed chinchilla, has the smaller, leaner build but also the silkier coat. The *brevicaudata*, or short-tailed chinchilla, has the coarser coat and larger, blockier appearance. Initially, breeders tried crossing the two species to produce a more hardy chinchilla—one that had the size of the *brevicaudata* and the coat of the *lanigera*—however, this project stalled when breeders found that offspring from these lines were sterile. Domestic chinchillas were then bred primarily from the *lanigera* species, and today, domestic chinchillas are classified as being of this species, even though they may appear to carry some *brevicaudata* traits as well. The blocky *brevicaudata* body type seen in show chinchillas, for example, although to some extent a result of limited crossbreeding of species, has come about primarily through selective breeding.

Chinchilla Characteristics

Type/ Species	Brevicaudata/ Brevicaudata	Lanigera/ Lanigera	Costina/ Lanigera
Altitude	High: 11,500–16,000 ft	Medium: 10,000 ft	Low: 1,000–10,000 ft
Ears/Nose	Short/Flat	Medium/Blunt	Long/Pointed
Tail	Short	Long	Long
Body/Fur	Chunky and compact, good conformation, with long, thick fur that has poor texture	Lean, good conformation, with long, thick fur	Slim, with short fur that has good texture and dark color, but poor clarity
Size	Large: more than 24 oz	Medium: 16–24 oz	Small: less than 20 oz
Breeding Abilities	Poor	Poor	Prolific

Another distinct chinchilla type is the *costina*. Scientists have determined that the *costina*, once thought to be perhaps a third chinchilla species, is a variant of the *lanigera;* chinchilla folk still make a distinction between the two. The differences between *costina* and *lanigera* (for example, the *costina*'s smaller, slimmer build and longer ears) are attributed to the *costina's* adaptations to living at lower altitudes. The *costina* is the smallest and most streamlined of the three but also the most prolific

A baby viscacha stretches as her mother snoozes. Viscachas are a close relative of the chinchilla, but much larger in size.

producer. Both *lanigera* and *costina* were represented among the chinchillas that first arrived in the United States and established this country's original line of domestic chinchillas.

The closest relative of the chinchilla, also in the Chinchillidae family, is the viscacha. With its orange fur, long ears, broad nose, and narrow face, it is even stranger looking than its close cousin—almost a Dr. Seuss–like caricature of the chinchilla!

Unrodent-like Rodents

Even though chinchillas are classified as rodents, they are in many ways not rodentlike at all. One of their unrodent-like characteristics is their long life span. Chinchillas typically live ten to fifteen years; with the right breeding and care, you may have your chinchillas for up to twenty years. And whereas the typical rodent is a baby-producing machine, a female chinchilla bears few offspring in her lifetime. At the end of a very long gestation period (lasting 111 to 119 days—which is longer than a dog's or a cat's), she will deliver only one or two babies, maybe three. In her prime, she will have about two litters a year. Finally, chinchillas differ from other rodents in that they are highly intelligent animals with a complex verbal and nonverbal communication structure and the ability to learn and even mimic the communications of other animals. They can understand some human words, too.

Because chinchillas come from South America, I've always thought a girl should be called a chinchilla and a boy a chinchillo (babies could be called chinlets!). Technically, though, chinchillas share gender names, as is fitting, with the shy, gentle, wide-eyed deer: the females are called does and the males, bucks. Chinchilla babies, however, are called kits, not fawns.

Wild Origins

The wild ancestors of pet chinchillas originated in the mountains of Argentina, Bolivia, Chile, and Peru, where the weather is very cool year-round and where wild chinchillas still live today. The Chinca Indians wore coats made of the animal's fur, and when the Europeans arrived on the scene, they called these animals *chinchillas*, which means "little Chincas." The Europeans' eventual conquest of the region meant not only the demise of the Chincas but the downfall of the *little* Chincas as well. Chinchilla numbers dwindled from millions to thousands as the Europeans hunted them for their fur, almost to the brink of extinction.

Fortunately, in 1910, the governments of Argentina, Bolivia, Chile, and Peru banded together and outlawed the trapping of wild chinchillas. These countries have made repeated attempts since then to reestablish wild chinchilla populations. Some of the most successful chinchilla herds live on animal preserves within these countries. But chinchillas in the wild continue to struggle for survival as humans invade and alter the animals' natural habitat.

Chinchillas, being from a dry climate, drink and urinate very little and therefore are practically odorless. They once lived in large herds that could number up to 100 members, most

Like most chinchillas, this one is amazingly agile and enjoys nothing better than running at top speed.

inhabiting burrows, some taking up residence in crevices. Chinchillas don't have many natural defense mechanisms and so protect themselves by fleeing, which they do well. They are fast and, given their size, surprisingly silent, and they can jump distances several times their body height. When danger arises, they bark a warning to the rest of the herd and, if cornered, will fire a stream of urine spot-on in the faces of would-be predators (young females are especially adept at this). If chinchillas are grabbed, they have the ability to "slip" or "blow" their fur, releasing a portion of it from the roots to loosen the predator's grip, much to the surprise of the predator. How much fur is lost depends on how scared the chinchillas are.

Although chinchillas are usually quiet, they can make noises that are as varied and unusual as their looks—they can bleat in contentment, spit in anger, bark in excitement, or honk in annoyance. Their diet in the wild consists of plants, fruits, seeds, and insects. Interestingly, any attempts to replicate the wild diet with captive chinchillas has led to serious, often fatal illness; unlike their wild ancestors, domestic chinchillas are strict herbivores and thrive on a restricted menu of pellets, dried hay, and a few raw grains.

Names for Chinchillas

Official name: **Chinchilla, *a Spanish word meaning "little Chincas"***

Nicknames: chinchillas, chins, chinnies

Official classification: **Chinchilla lanigera, *doe (girl), buck (boy), kit (baby)***

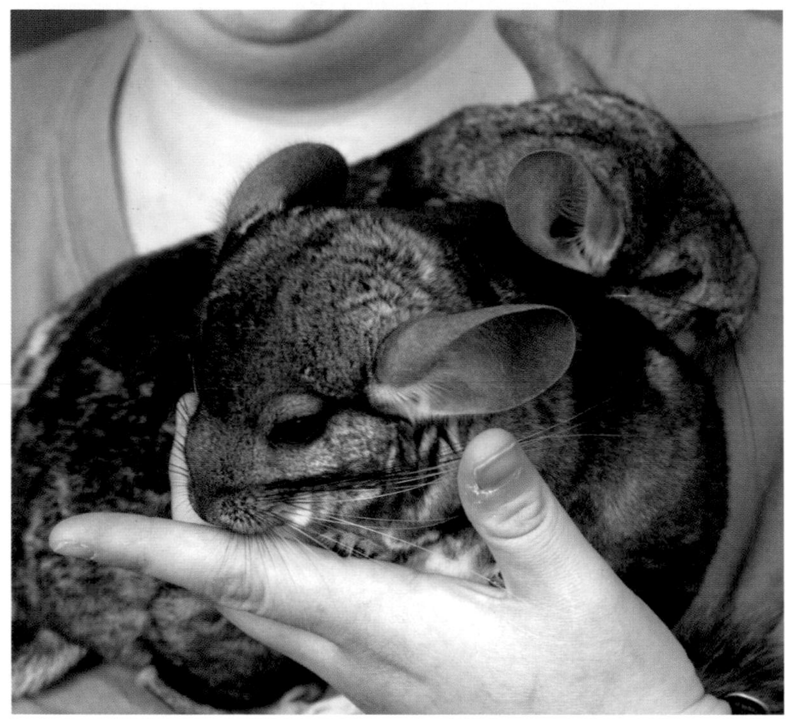

These chinchilla roommates are the best of friends.

Coming to the United States

At the same time as the South American governments began their struggle to save the wild chinchilla, a Californian named Mathias Chapman became interested in establishing a ranch of captive chinchillas in the United States. It took him many years to achieve his goal: first, he had to convince the South American countries to agree to his plan. Then, he had to catch wild chinchillas suitable for breeding and very gradually acclimate them to a warmer, lower altitude. And finally, he had to find a way to transport them to the United States, which wasn't easy—he ended up sneaking the animals on board past the ship's captain and icing their housing all the way to keep them cooled. All eleven captured chinchillas—three females and eight males—survived their arduous travels, and Mathias Chapman became the first U.S. chinchilla rancher. It wasn't too long before it was discovered that these animals not only are beautifully furred, but once they have built a trust with a person, can also be graceful, inquisitive, intelligent, and affectionate companions.

Color Varieties

Although some pet chinchillas are larger than others—they range from under a pound to well over 2 pounds (from 10½ to 35 ounces)—they nevertheless come in just one size variety (no dwarf or giant pet chinchillas), one body type (no lop-eared or tailless chinchillas), and one coat type (no longhaired, rex, or

This chinchilla, like most other chinchillas bred as pets, has the same beautiful Standard Gray coloring that chinchillas in the wild have.

hairless). The most obvious difference among chinchillas is color: many varieties have been established. The most common color by far is Standard Gray, which is the natural (wild) chinchilla coat color, usually coupled with a white belly. About 90 percent of all pet chinchillas are the Standard Gray. Colors other than Standard Gray are called color mutations. The first of these arose in the 1950s as a result of selective breeding; called Wilson White, it was characterized by a pure white fur with gray ears and black eyes. Chinchillas now come in many additional colors, from jet black all over to beige, tan, chocolate, and violet. Touch

The white color of this chinchilla's coat is a result of selective breeding; white was the first color variation created by breeders.

History of Chinchilla Color Mutations

DOMINANT MUTATIONS—only one parent needs to carry the trait to pass it on:

- ***Wilson White, 1955***
- ***Tower Beige or Dominant Beige, 1960***
- ***Gunning Black, also called Black Velvet or the original Touch of Velvet (TOV), 1960–1961***
- ***Tasco Black or Ebony, 1964***
- ***Tan, mid-1960s***

RECESSIVE MUTATIONS—both parents must pass the trait on to the offspring for the color to occur. These are rarer, in general, and include:

- ***Wellman Beige, 1954 (dark eyes)***
- ***Recessive Beige or Sullivan Beige (red eyes), late 1950s***
- ***Pink White (white with pink ears and red eyes), 1960***
- ***Charcoal, early 1960s***
- ***Sapphire, 1963–1965***
- ***Sullivan Violet or Lavender, sometimes referred to as just Violet, 1967***
- ***Lavender Brown, 1969***
- ***Lester Black (dark to jet-black, including belly), 1970***

Countless other color mutations can be created by breeding two different mutations; for example, Black Velvet bred with Tan can produce Touch of Velvet Tan.

Source: Basic Genetics and History of Mutation Chinchillas *by Alice Kline*

of Velvet mutations have darker fur on a face mask, along the back, and on paw bands. Patches of color rather than even coloring is called Mosaic.

CHAPTER

2

The Perfect Pet?

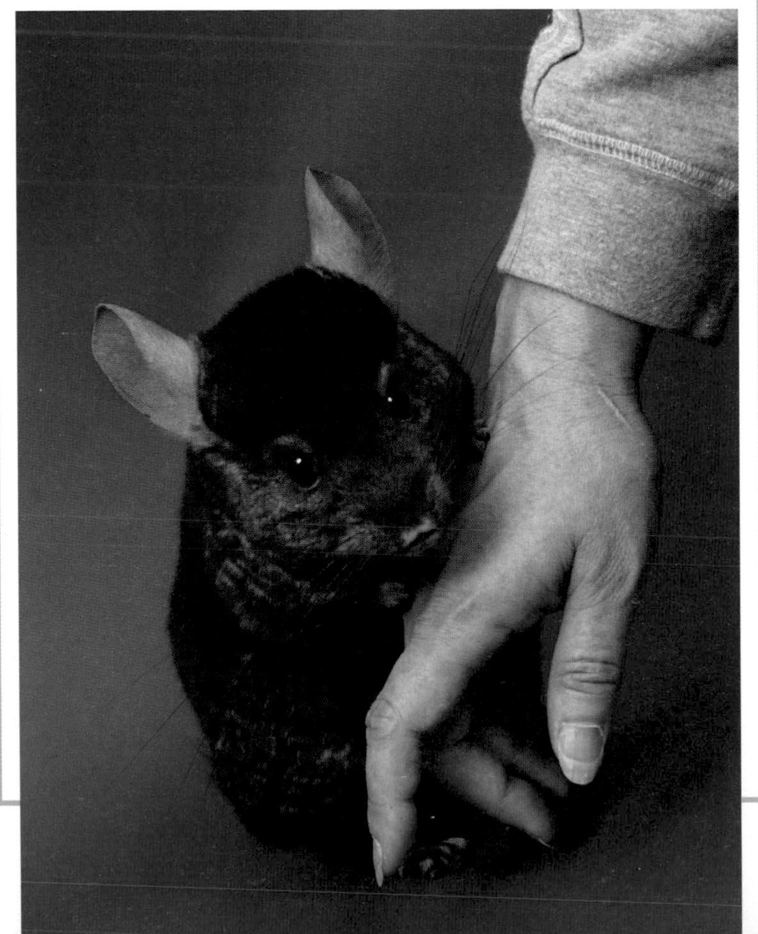

This trusting chinchilla relaxes in his owner's arms.

AT FIRST GLANCE, ONE MAY WONDER WHY PEOPLE KEEP chinchillas as pets at all. They are rather shy animals that sleep in the day; they are stressed out by the normal hustle and bustle of daily living; and despite being the softest animals on earth, they don't really like being stroked and petted. Look a little deeper, though, and you'll discover the secret known to those who keep these unusual animals: chinchillas are not only exotic looking, athletic, agile, silent, and practically odorless, but once you've earned their trust, they are also affectionate and playful companions. For the right individual, these are very cool pets—engaging, fun, and relatively easy to keep. The key to establishing a happy chinchilla-person relationship is to set the right expectations and, ideally, as few as possible.

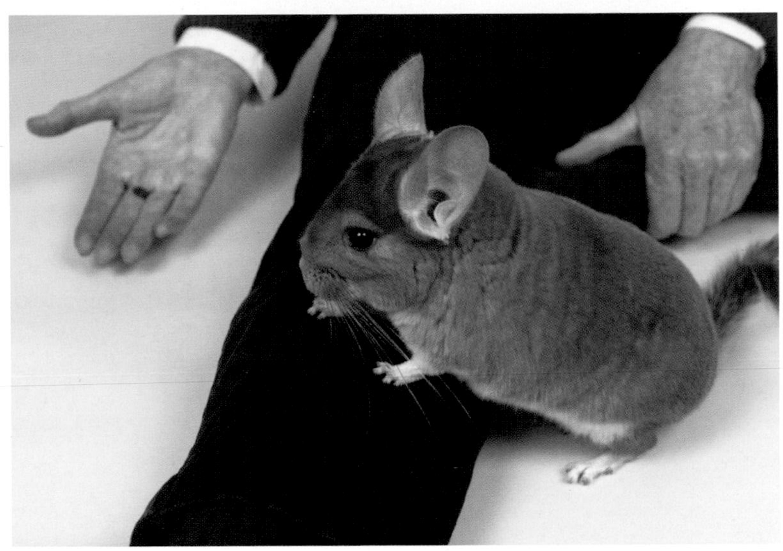

A chinchilla has some fun with his owner. Chinchillas like to have their people watch them at play.

Are You Right for Chins?

The would-be chinchilla owner needs to appreciate the personality of the animal and not expect it to be different from what it is. First, you cannot expect the chinchilla to be like a cat, which will curl up and fall asleep in your lap, or like a dog, which will lie down at your feet. Chinchillas are animals on the move. Second, they are one-person or one-family animals. You won't be able to parade them in front of your friends or show off their antics to your family. As soon as a stranger enters the room, most chinchillas will retreat into the back corner of the cage and keep a wary eye on this potential threat. And finally, the ideal chinchilla person is one who can keep the chins on a routine, is typically home for some part of the evening, and doesn't travel too much. Chinchillas thrive under a predictable pattern of feeding, playtime, and attention.

Bonding Time

It can take your chinchillas several weeks or even up to six months of positive, daily interaction to become fully tame and bonded with you. During that time, they will be watching your every motion, listening to your every sound, and remembering each treat and kindness bestowed. Slowly, they will relax their natural wariness and eventually transform (or so it will seem) into new creatures. Whereas at first they either remained still and reserved or took flight at your arrival, now they shove their noses through the wire holes as you approach with a treat or shamelessly fling themselves against the bars of the cage as the appointed free run time draws near. Once out of the cage, they frequently come to visit, almost making a nuisance of themselves, rummaging through your front pocket, remembering past treat spots even you've forgotten. The more you laugh at their antics—such as their leaping from floor to lap to back of recliner chair to bookshelf to floor—the more they repeat the trick again and again, just to amuse you.

This chinchilla perches comfortably on his owner's shoulder. Clearly, he has forged a deep bond with the special person in his life.

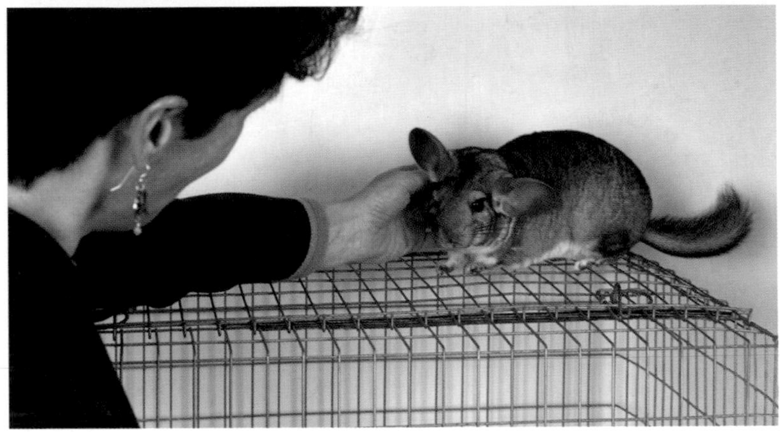

This chinchilla loves to be scratched under the chin and behind the ears. Observe your chinchilla to see where and how much he wants to be petted.

It is no wonder that many people end up with not only their original chinchillas but a small herd of their own!

Expect Cute but Not Cuddly

If you are looking for a pet to pet, don't be deceived by the chin's cuddly coat, or you might be in for a disappointment. Chinchilla fur is amazingly dense and soft, and it's no wonder. People have one hair growing out of each follicle, whereas chinchillas have fifty to sixty! One look at that luxurious coat, and your natural tendency is to grab the chinchilla right up, burrow your fingers into that thick fur, and cuddle the soft little creature close. Here is the ironic part: most chinchillas hate this sort of treatment. Chinchillas are sensitive animals of prey with fragile bones; they are afraid of quick motions and of being grabbed. Even being stroked or touched, especially on the back, can make a chinchilla feel vulnerable. And while some chins may be comfortable enough to be held close and petted, they'll soon feel too warm, given that heavy coat, and will wriggle to get away.

This isn't to say you can never hold your chinchillas. Shake a box of raisins, and a chinchilla or two will be sitting on your lap in no time. The trick is to let your chinchillas come to you—have *them* teach *you* just how much and what type of contact they want. Many love to be scratched on the cheek, ears, chest, and behind the front paws. Take the time to discover just exactly what your own unique chinchillas love. Does the one turn his head and close his eyes when you find just the right spot behind his ear? Does the other chitter and scold when you touch her tail but nuzzle up for a chest rub? It is a special moment when you discover just the right touch.

The Need to Handle with Care

Chinchillas have light bones that are easily broken. Improper housing and rough handling are the two main ways chinchillas suffer broken limbs. (Note that a broken leg often can and should be set by a veterinarian and will heal). The chinchilla is not considered a sturdy animal and so is not usually a suitable pet for a young child.

A pet owner holds his chinchilla securely against his body, while being careful to protect the chinchilla's delicate bones.

Holding a chinchilla is more like handling a bird than handling a typical mammal—hold your hands out still, or carefully scoop the animal up from underneath and let it perch on you. A nervous or struggling chinchilla that must be picked up should be held firmly, but without squeezing, close up against your body; the frightened animal will gain confidence and comfort from your self-assuredness.

Commit for the Long Haul

Most people who give up their chinchillas do so because of a lifestyle change: for example, a family moves and cannot take the chinchillas along, or a teenage owner goes to college and the parents want to travel and don't want pets. Another common scenario is that a cute chinchilla in the pet store window is bought on impulse; the new owner doesn't have time for the animal, only realizes it after the fact, and ends up giving the chin away. Our society tends to have a "disposable pets" mentality. Given the chinchilla's long life span and the bond this animal develops with primary caretakers, it is better not to shuffle chins from one home to the next. Think about where you will be in ten, fifteen, or even twenty years before committing to owning chinchillas.

What's Involved in Keeping Chinchillas

Before acquiring chinchillas, it is important to understand not only what to expect from this unique animal but also the responsibilities, cost, and commitment involved. The initial outlay will be greater for a chinchilla than for other small pets. And you will need to provide chinchillas with a living environment that is cool and not too chaotic. However, once you're set up, you'll find that the upkeep of these animals is affordable and relatively easy.

The Cost

Because chinchillas are social, getting a pair is best. A pair of Standard Gray chinchillas and a large cage and supplies will cost about $500. The cost could be twice that much, depending on how fancy the chinchillas' coloring is and how elaborate the housing and extras are. Although this is a big initial expense, you will have your chinchillas for many years, and they are inexpensive to feed and keep and unlikely to require veterinary care other than routine preventive checkups. That said, it is recommended that you have $200 on reserve. Should your chinchilla ever fall ill or become injured, you'll need this reserve fund to cover an office visit and to pay for medications and treatment (chinchillas are considered exotics, which can mean "expensive").

Start-up Costs

Pair of chinchillas: $150 (Standard Gray); more for rarer colored or show-quality pair
Quality cage (includes shipping): prices start at $150
Nest box: $25
Stand (optional): $50
Exercise wheel or saucer (optional): $50–$75
Wellness visit (optional): $50
Three-month supply of litter and food: $25
Dust bath house or bowl and chinchilla dust: $20
Ceramic food dish and water bottle: $15
Toy and chew block: $15
Total cost: $500 and up

Cheer up! Chinchillas are expensive to buy but inexpensive to keep—only pennies a day to feed.

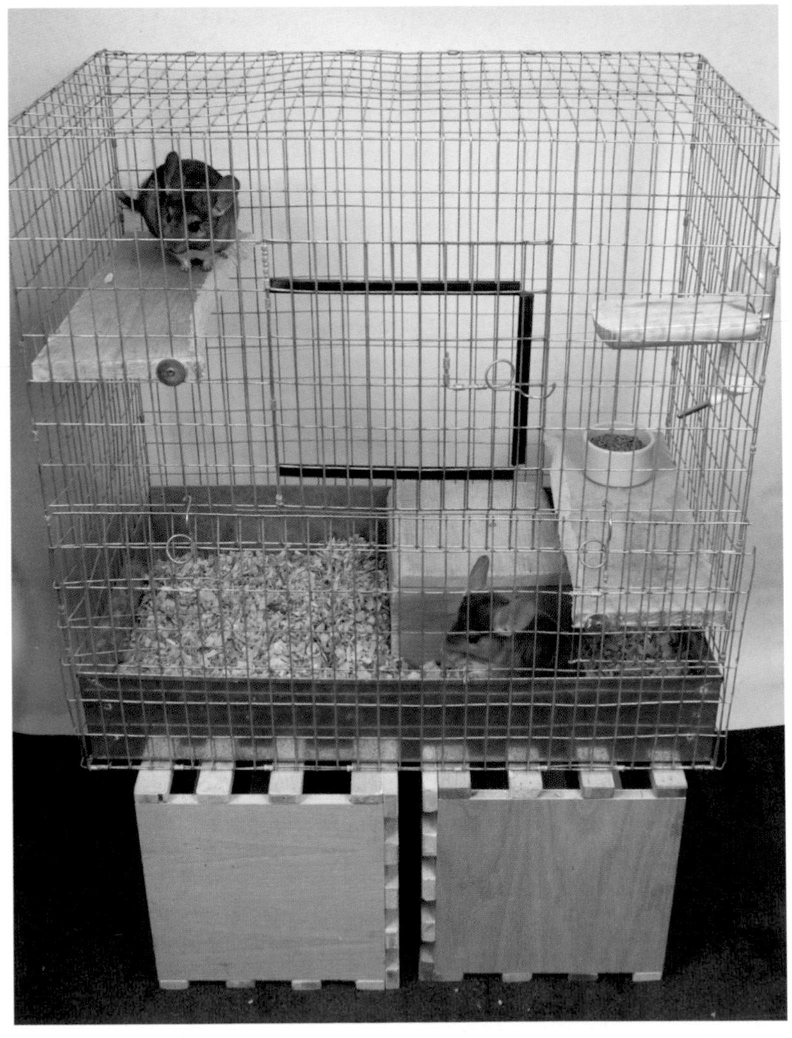

Buying a used cage in good condition, such as this one, can reduce the initial cost of chinchilla ownership.

If the only thing standing between you and chinchillas is the cost, work with a local humane society or rescue group, or try http://www.petfinder.com. Often, the adoption fee is reasonable, and they may have a used housing setup available, too. With persistence, you can find friendly chinchillas looking for a caring second home. Another possibility is to work with a breeder who wants to place a retired breeding pair.

The Time Investment in Chin Care

I would say that the time required for a chinchilla is more than it is for the low-maintenance gerbil but less than it is for the high-maintenance rat or ferret. Chinchillas are very easy to feed, and like gerbils, they urinate very little, making cage cleaning a breeze. Chinchillas can be characterized as medium-maintenance small pets (similar to guinea pigs or rabbits), with the good news being that most of the time you'll spend with them is in interacting and play, rather than in taking care of their basic needs.

Chinchillas are not needy animals. This is a huge plus for a person who enjoys the company of animals but wouldn't want one that is too demanding of time or is constantly begging for undivided attention. If you get into the habit of giving them free runs in the evening, your chinchillas will expect this as part of the routine. Even during playtime, though, they are more than content to let you read a book, watch TV, or work on the computer, as long as they can come over occasionally to sneak a nibble of a page corner or dash across the keyboard, typing you a nonsensical message.

Another time commitment, in addition to playtime, is the time needed to carry out husbandry chores. Although a chinchilla cage would take a very long time to become smelly, it should be cleaned out weekly, which is likely to take about a half hour. Providing pellets, timothy hay, and fresh water takes just a few minutes a day. Chinchillas should also be given frequent opportunities to take a dust bath (which means rolling in chinchilla dust—see chapter 5 for more on this). All chinchillas love a dust bath.

Keep It Cool

Probably the biggest obstacle to keeping chinchillas is that they need to be kept cool at all times. To keep a chinchilla, you need to live in a cool climate or in a home that has air-conditioning or an underground, finished basement where your chinchillas can live (provided it's not damp). Remember that chinchillas wear thick fur coats year-round. They do best in temperatures between 65 and 70 degrees—in fact, they would set the thermostat to the 50s if they could reach it! Chinchillas should never be exposed to temperatures higher than 79 degrees Fahrenheit.

Not only temperature but also humidity can affect chinchillas. High humidity in combination with high temperature is especially dangerous to them. A dehumidifier is another way to help keep things cool. (See chapter 3 for more details on temperature control and warm weather issues.)

Not Kid Stuff

Chinchillas are not good pets for young children. It is important, in dealing with chinchillas, to speak softly, make slow steady movements, read their reactions, respect the fact that they may be stressed or afraid, and refrain from picking them up and petting them, except as they invite and enjoy such handling. Any one of these behaviors may be hard for a child to understand or follow. That said, when closely supervised, young children may enjoy watching a parent's chinchillas leap from ledge to ledge in their cage, feeding them Cheerios, or taking on the challenge of sitting very still and silent next to Mom or Dad to see if the animals will alight on them. A chinchilla can be a wonderful pet for a quiet, gentle, patient teenager or an exceptionally mature preteen. As with any pets purchased for kids, a responsible adult should make sure the animals have food and water every day, live in a clean cage, and receive proper care and handling.

Housekeeping Issues

One disadvantage to keeping chinchillas is that they are poop dispensers. Wherever they go, a trail of droppings follows. Don't even think about potty training them; while they're usually good about peeing in their chosen corner, when it comes to pooping, they don't seem the least bit aware that it is happening as they run along! In their cage, piles of droppings appear on the ledges and get flung out of the cage. The good news is that because chinchillas are herbivores that eat a simple diet of alfalfa-based pellets and timothy hay, their droppings are hard and odorless and can be vacuumed right up. A small shop vacuum or hand vacuum to keep right next to the cage or in their play room might be a good investment.

Although they poop a lot, they pee very little, making them practically odorless pets. Their urine is also restricted to a favorite spot in the cage, and they rarely, if ever, urinate when out of the cage, particularly if you keep their romps to no more than a couple of hours and leave the cage door open.

One more thing: when out playing, chinchillas love to chew up your stuff—and the furniture, fixtures, carpets, and walls as well!

Where to Find Your Chinchillas

Once you've decided you want pet chinchillas, you have a few choices of places to get them: pet stores, rescue shelters, breeders' kennels, or chinchilla ranches.

Chinchillas in the Schools?

Do chinchillas make good classroom pets? Well, perhaps for a small, adult night class of introverted adults—other than this, it is hard to imagine a worse environment for chinchillas! During the day, they need a quiet, calm home to sleep in, and in the evening, gentle and consistent care from one or a few individuals they've come to know and trust. Daytime activity, yelling youngsters, and poking fingers all add up to one very stressed-out chinchilla.

Pet Stores

Not all pet stores are ideal places to get chinchillas. Because chinchillas are expensive pets, they often spend quite some time in the pet store before being purchased. During the day, while trying to sleep, the nocturnal chinchilla is surrounded by bright light and noise. At night, when the chin is up and ready to play, there are no humans about to interact with and no large areas to run about in and explore. Chinchillas do better when they have a dedicated person caring for them and can bond to people early in life.

Avoid pet stores that keep chinchillas in tanks, rather than in well-ventilated wire cages, and in areas that provide too small a living space. The cages should have ledges for leaping to and from and wheels for running on.

Chinchilla Rescue Shelters

A chinchilla or animal rescue organization might have chinchillas for adoption. Another resource is http://www.petfinder.com. It is especially important when adopting from shelters to spend time with the chinchillas and talk with their caretakers about any issues the animals may have. It is best to leave "problem chinchillas" to experienced chinchilla keepers. Like their wild relatives, these animals initially might bite or spray urine in an attempt to take charge or drive people away. A novice to chinchillas is unlikely to know how to handle such situations. However, sometimes family circumstances force the surrender of friendly, well-socialized chinchillas that make wonderful pets for a first-time chinchilla keeper. Many chinchillas that end up in shelters were purchased on impulse from a pet store as babies and are less than a year old.

When you adopt from a chinchilla rescue organization, the staff will ask you to fill out an adoption application form (some breeders will do this as well). See the Chinchilla Adoption Application Form on page 39 for the types of questions you could be asked. Rescue organizations may also provide an educational home visit. A staff member will come out to your home to give family members the opportunity to ask questions and to make sure that you have the right supplies for the chinchilla, a suitable cage and housing location, and accurate care expectations and that there are no hazards to the chinchilla in your home. One option a rescue organization may offer is a "foster first" arrangement for families that are new to keeping pets. All of these precautions are taken so that the chinchilla will find a permanent home and not be bounced from place to place.

It is not necessary to get chinchillas as babies for them to bond with you. There are benefits to acquiring chinchillas both as babies and as young adults. The most obvious benefit with babies is that they are unbelievably adorable. You can also give them plenty of gentle handling when they need it most. The personality of a baby chinchilla is still developing, though, so if you are looking for a certain kind of chinchilla—very outgoing, for example, or very gentle—you may be better off adopting young adults whose personalities are already formed. Since chinchillas usually live from ten to fifteen years, you will still have many, many years to enjoy the companionship of your new pets.

Maybe you would like chinchillas but aren't quite sure you want that long a commitment. If so, opening your home to a pair of older chinchillas will have certain advantages. Older chinchillas may also be less expensive and, given time, should bond nicely with you.

Chinchilla Breeders

Another place to acquire your chinchillas is from a breeder of pet chinchillas. You will be able to meet the parents of the chinchillas you are interested in; often, the offspring will have a

You can see adorable babies, such as this tiny chin, if you visit a chinchilla breeder.

Chinchilla Ranches

Some people acquire fine pets from chinchilla ranches, but unless this is the only way to get a chinchilla of the color or quality you want, I'd recommend against it. It would be better to support establishments that breed chinchillas as pets rather than for their fur. Often, pet chinchilla breeders choose animals from ranch or show lines, so the quality of the animals is comparable. It would be wiser, too, to adopt animals that have been housed in roomier quarters than a ranch provides and have had a more stimulating environment and more opportunity for positive human contact from the start. If you do decide to adopt your chinchillas from a fur rancher, your pets will require special care as they transition to their new housing and environment (described in chapter 4). Unless you give them this special transitioning care, you may lose them to stress or self-injury.

temperament very like that of one of the parents. A responsible breeder who has raised several generations of chinchillas will have bred out the more serious genetic issues, such as heart murmur and malocclusion (although such defects can pop up in any herd). Another advantage in buying from a breeder is that you will know the exact age of the chinchillas and know that they have been handled lovingly and properly from birth.

Finding a Breeder

One way to find a breeder is to get a referral from a chinchilla owner with very nice chinchillas. The ones you adopt may have different personalities but should be as tame and healthy if they come from the same line. Following are three good online resources that provide breeder listings:

- Chinchilla Club breeder directory at http://www.chinchillaclub.com/breeder/
- Pets On The Net chinchilla breeders at http://www.pets-on-the-net.com/directory/chinchilla/
- Chinchilla Yellow Pages at http://www.etc-etc.com/yellowpg.htm

What to Ask and Observe

Start off by having a discussion on the phone with a chinchilla breeder and talk about yourself and the breeder's program and chins. The breeder may be able to send you pictures of available babies. See if you can set up a time to meet the parents of newborn or upcoming babies, as their temperament and health will tell you something about what to expect when your babies grow up.

When you see the babies (or available adults), you should look for these qualities:

- Eyes are bright
- Energy level is high
- Fur is soft, smooth, and shiny
- Behavior is friendly, not withdrawn or nervous

The breeder will expect and want you to ask intelligent and caring questions about the chins you will adopt. Breeders want to make sure the chinchillas are going to good homes where they will be well cared for. Write down a list of questions, and ask them all at once rather than sending several e-mails or making calls as the questions come up; chinchilla breeders tend to be busy people. Here are some questions you may want to ask:

- What kinds of food are the chinchillas eating? The breeder may offer to give or sell you some to take home and let you

Chinchilla Adoption Application Form

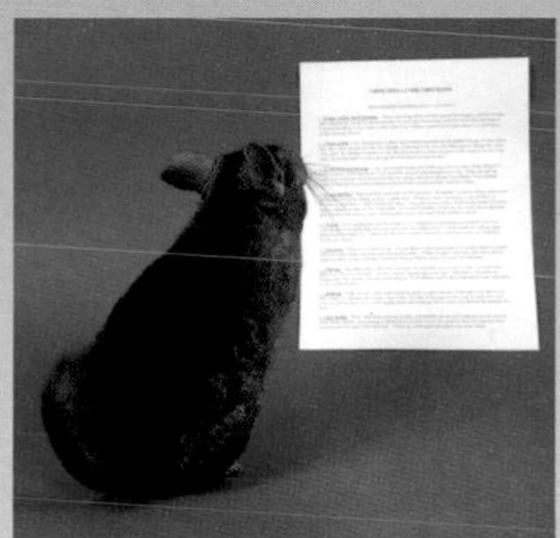

A chinchilla scans a take-home care sheet for completeness.

- ***Provide information on whether you rent, the rental property's pet policy, and the landlord's contact information.***
- ***Do you plan to move in the coming years, and if so, what will you do with the chinchilla?***
- ***List the ages of any children in the home.***
- ***Who will be responsible for the care and cost of the chinchilla?***
- ***Give a description of the caging/housing you will provide for the chinchilla.***
- ***Will you allow the chinchilla to go outside of its cage? Why or why not?***
- ***What will you feed the chinchilla?***
- ***Which veterinarian do you plan to take the chinchilla to? Provide contact information.***
- ***How many hours per day will the chinchilla be without human companionship?***
- ***How often do you travel?***
- ***If you go away, who will take care of the chinchilla?***
- ***Do you have any other pets? If so, please list the names, species, and ages.***

Source: Small Animal Rescue Society of British Columbia (http://www.smallanimalrescue.org)

know where to buy more. Some breeders even put together a small care package of food, hay or hay cubes, and supplement for you to take home.

- Does the breeder post care information online or provide a care sheet?
- Will the breeder spend time teaching a first-time chinchilla keeper? (A good breeder will want to make sure the animals receive the right care.)
- Can you visit the parents? Some breeders may not want you to go into the breeding room, lest you introduce germs or upset the herd with lots of foot traffic; others will let you go in.
- To avoid misunderstandings, it is a good idea to see that all agreements are put in writing and signed by both adopter and adoptee.

What a Breeder Will Expect from You

Breeders will also have certain expectations from those interested in the chinchillas. You should know the chin basics—you should be aware that they live a long time, for example, and know how to house and feed them. The breeder will expect you to ask for certain important information, as well:

- Guidelines on where to put the cage
- Information about which available accessories are good (and safe) and which are gimmicks
- Recommendations regarding diet and which food and hay brands to buy
- Tips on chinchilla behavior
- Taming and training ideas
- Recommendations for a good chinchilla veterinarian

Once you have chosen a breeder, the breeder may want you to bring your pets' housing so he or she can see where the chins will live. If you plan to use a cat carrier to transport the chins home, clean it thoroughly; otherwise, it will be a health issue—and will make a bad impression, too.

Adopting Healthy Chinchillas

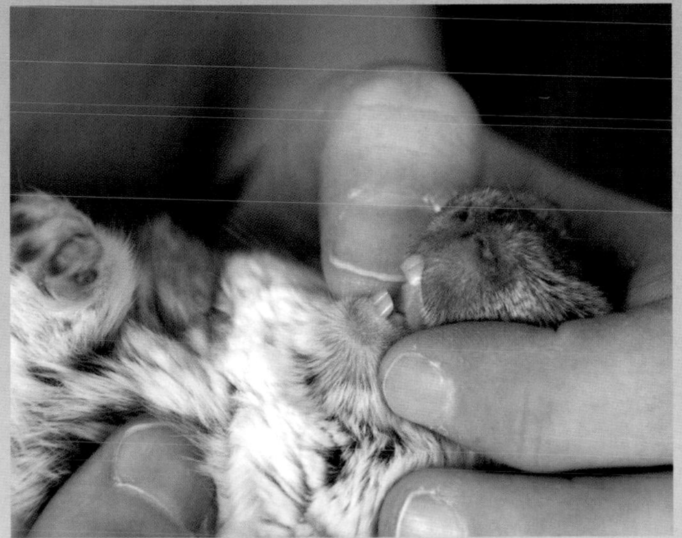

Healthy adult teeth, such as those shown here between the owner's thumb and forefinger, are yellow and are not overgrown or misaligned.

NO MATTER WHERE YOU GET YOUR CHINS, YOU WANT TO make sure they are healthy. Two important health issues to watch for are malocclusion and heart murmur. Malocclusion is a rare genetic condition in which the back or front teeth don't align and so cannot be ground down by gnawing. (See chapter 8 for more on malocclusion.) This problem shows up in chinchillas when they are about eighteen months old. One way to help avoid malocclusion is to adopt babies from older parents. If the parents have been producing babies for years without malocclusion being an issue, it is likely that the babies you purchase will be problem free, too. A heart murmur is another potentially serious problem that can be passed from parents to babies. Working with a well-established breeder who has raised several problem-free generations is a good way to avoid seeing either problem in the chins you adopt.

Choosing a Chinchilla

Now that you have found a place with healthy chinchillas for adoption, you have several more decisions to make: How many chinchillas? Boys or girls? What color? Think carefully, too, about what sort of chinchilla temperament and personality traits will best suit you and your lifestyle.

Two Chins May Be Better Than One

As mentioned earlier, getting two chinchillas is recommended. Being a herd animal by nature, a chinchilla feels safer having

Neutering

THE DECISION TO NEUTER A CHINCHILLA SHOULD NOT BE taken lightly. For the most part, there is no behavioral or medical need for your chinchilla to be neutered (or spayed, if it's a girl). If you choose to do so, the risks should be carefully considered in consultation with a veterinarian experienced in performing this procedure on this animal (ask about the veterinarian's numbers and success rate). Neutering a chinchilla is a delicate procedure because administering anesthesia to such a sensitive animal can be touchy; aftereffects can still show up even weeks later. The stress, combined with the surgery itself, can make neutering a chinchilla dangerous or fatal. Taking extra post-op measures, such as keeping the cage mate nearby when the chinchilla is waking up and giving the neutered chin painkillers, may help manage stress. It will take about a week to ten days for the incision to heal, and during that time, you may want to house the neutered male alone in a single level cage, located right next to his cage mate. Make sure to watch him carefully when you return him to his partner. Spaying a female chinchilla is a much more complicated surgery and is not recommended unless it is deemed medically necessary.

another of its kind around. And being an active and intelligent animal that is awake all night, a chinchilla enjoys having a playmate to interact with while the rest of the household is asleep. Even during the day, while awake but resting, my chinchillas like to rest sitting side by side on the top ledge. Just having a companion in a nearby cage is often enough to comfort a lone chinchilla.

Girls or Boys?

Boys or girls make equally good pets; girls tend to be a bit more rambunctious than boys, and boys are more likely than girls to quarrel among themselves. A lot depends on the individual chinchilla's unique personality. If not raised together, a paired adult and youngster or two adult chinchillas need to be introduced to each other gradually and carefully, as discussed in more detail in the next chapter. If you get two youngsters, you can easily pair

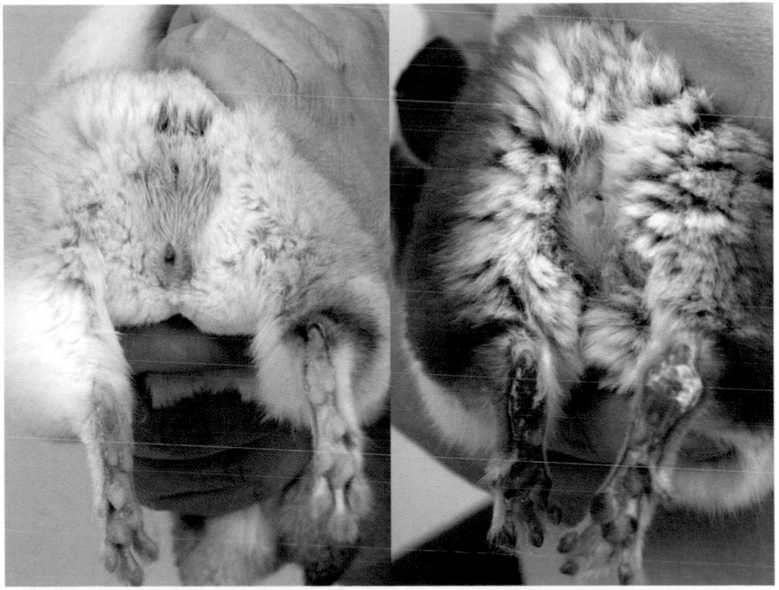

The genitalia on a male chinchilla, shown above left, are more separated. A female chinchilla's genitalia, shown above right, are almost touching.

either two girls or two boys, and they should get along fine when they grow up. You could also keep mother with daughter or father with son (that is, if the dad stayed with the mom and helped raise his offspring). Introducing chinchillas as adults is easier if you have girls. If you have a boy and he is lonely, you could introduce him to a girl and neuter him if you do not want babies.

What Color?

Color is a personal preference. The cost and availability of chinchillas depends on both their color and the darkness of the color (darker chinchillas are rarer and more costly). The chart on color availability will give you an idea of how easy or diffi-

Here are some examples of chinchilla color varieties.

Color Availability

Names	Description	Cost and Availability
Standard or Standard Gray	Body – gray in many shades. Belly – white. Eyes – black. Ears – gray or black.	$75 Easy to find
Hetero Beige or Beige	Body – beige. Belly – white. Eyes – red. Ears – pink.	$125 Easy
Homo Beige or Light Beige	Body – very pale beige. Belly – white. Eyes – red. Ears – pink.	$150–$300 Medium
Pink White or White	Body – mostly white with beige patches. Belly – white. Eyes – red. Ears – pink.	$150 Medium
Wilson White or White	Body – white. Belly – white. Eyes – black. Ears – dark.	$150–$200 Easy
Another type of Wilson White: Mosaic	Body – gray and white. Belly – white. Eyes – black. Ears – gray.	$150 Medium
Another type of Wilson White: Silver	Body – white with gray fur tips. Belly – white. Eyes – black. Ears – gray.	$150–$200 Medium
Violet	Body – steel gray with a violet tinge. Belly – white. Eyes – black. Ears – pink to gray.	$200 Medium
Violet Touch of Velvet, Ultra Violet, or Violet Velvet	Body – gray with purple tinge; dark face mask, spine, and paw bands. Belly – white. Eyes – black. Ears – dark.	$250 Hard
Black Touch of Velvet, or Black Velvet	Body – gray with black mask and dark fur on neck and top of back; dark fur bands on front paws. Belly – white. Eyes – black. Ears – black.	$150 Medium

(cont.)

Names	*Description*	*Cost and Availability*
Brown Touch of Velvet, or Brown Velvet	*Body – gray with brown mask and fur on neck and top of back; brown fur bands on front paws. Belly – white. Eyes – red. Ears – pink.*	*$150–$200 Medium*
Charcoal	*Body – smoky gray in varying shades. Belly – matches body. Eyes – black. Ears – dark.*	*$100–$150 Medium*
Pastel	*Body – a color between beige and charcoal. Belly – matches body. Eyes – red. Ears – pink.*	*$150 Easy to medium*
Sapphire	*Body – dove gray with blue tinge. Belly – white. Eyes – black. Ears – dark.*	*$250–$300 Hard*
Ebony	*Body – gray to jet black. Belly – matches body. Eyes – black. Ears – dark.*	*Darker is rare and costs more. $100–$500 Easy to hard*
Tan	*Body – varies from a light to deep tan. Belly – matches body. Eyes – red. Ears – pink.*	*Darker is rare and costs more. $125–$300 Medium to hard*
Blue	*Body – gray with blue tinge. Belly – white. Eyes – black. Ears – gray.*	*$250–$500 Hard*
Chocolate	*Body – varies from milk chocolate ($250) to dark chocolate ($500). Belly – white. Eyes – black. Ears – dark.*	*$250–$500 Hard*

cult it may be to find a certain chinchilla color in the United States. Rather than setting your sights on a particular color, find a breeder that is highly recommended by other pet owners. Then, find out the colors he or she breeds, and pick from within those. Be flexible as well. If you visit the breeder and you bond instantly with a Standard Gray pair, that is probably the best choice all around. There is no difference in health or temperament based on color.

Personality Matters

When picking chinchillas, personality is by far the most important consideration. Decide on what you realistically want in terms of personality and what type of chinchilla will fit best into your lifestyle and schedule.

Most chinchillas are the independent sort; they love spending time with you but are happy to let you do your own stuff as they frolic in the area, popping over for the occasional visit. But some chinchillas are exceptionally outgoing and affectionate. They may be less content to be caged and more demanding of your attention when out of the cage, and some even enjoying sitting on your shoulder and accompanying you around the house. When seeking out the latter type, be prepared to dedicate the time needed to find the right breeder and to give these babies extensive handling as youngsters. Socializing chinchillas is similar to socializing puppies: if you want chinchillas that are especially good with people, it's important to introduce them while very young to a wide variety of people and to engage them in positive play sessions. Chinchillas handled lovingly and frequently from a very young age can overcome much of their natural wariness around people.

If selecting adult chinchillas, you may be better off visiting the breeder toward the evening, when the chins are fully awake. At first, sit quietly at a distance and watch as the animals interact with the breeder. You'll get a better idea of the temperament by doing this than by interacting directly with the animals, as their interactions with you would show how they react to strangers, as opposed to what their uninhibited personality is like. Chinchillas will like some people better than they like others. Consider letting the chinchilla pick you. If the breeder has a few chinchillas available, try handling each and see which ones seem to "click" best with you. Take your time. Chinchillas are naturally wary, so give them the chance to get over the initial introduction phase.

Many people want a chinchilla that will tolerate or enjoy at least some amount of handling. If this is what you want, it is important that you get an adult that is already interacting with people in this way.

Your other option, as mentioned earlier, is to carefully select a baby (again, primarily focusing on temperament, not worrying about color, gender, or other extraneous features). If the parents are jumping out into the breeder's hands, and the baby is already eager to come out and is comfortable with being held and carried around right from the start, you are well on your way to having a people-loving pet. Later, you can take full advantage of the chinchilla childhood and adolescent stages (see chapter 9) to tame your chin and give him or her lots of positive interaction with you and others.

Once you've made your decision and brought your chinchillas home, you need to respect, accept, appreciate, and enjoy them for who they are. Raising a chinchilla, like raising a child, is not about trying to make the chin something he or she is not

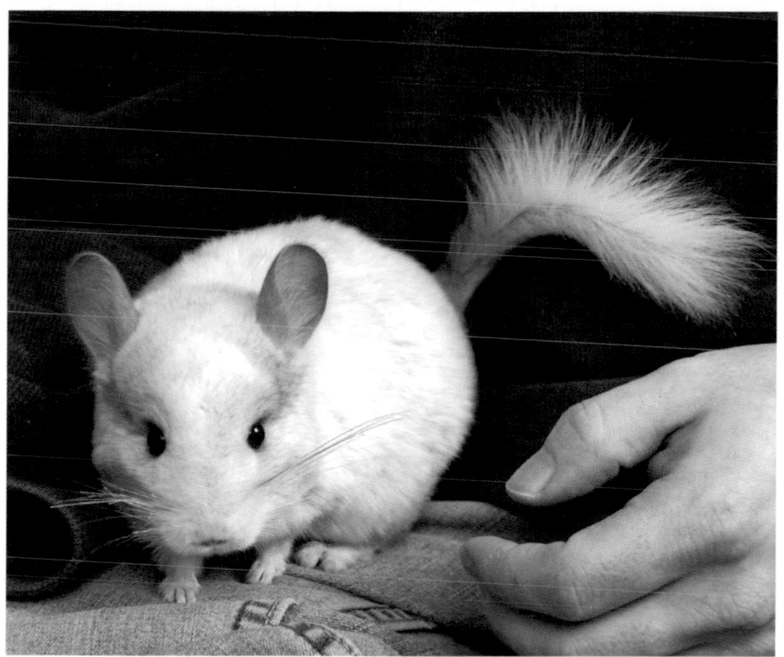

This adolescent Mosaic chinchilla sits happily on his owner's lap. When selecting a chinchilla, pick one that is friendly and confident.

but is all about enabling the animal to flourish and reach full chinchilla potential. You may find that one of your chinchillas (especially an adult changing homes for the second or third time) is not comfortable with being picked up but, over time, will scramble out of the cage to see you, sit on your lap and eat oats, and when play time is over, jump back into the cage with minimal herding. And that is perfectly OK, too.

CHAPTER

3

Housing and Accessories

Wait until your chinchillas are ten weeks old before taking them to their new home.

YOU'VE VISITED THE KENNEL, MET YOUR CHINCHILLAS' PARENTS (and perhaps grandparents, aunts, uncles, and cousins, too), and followed your little ones' progress through pictures and e-mail. The time is drawing near to bring your babies (no matter what their age) home. The best thing you can do for them is to make their homecoming as smooth and stress free as possible by setting up a perfect home for them well in advance and having everything prepared for their arrival.

Location, Location, Location

Placing the chinchilla cage in the right location is critical. The cage should be located in a relatively quiet area of the house, where the chinchillas can get a good day's sleep. A kitchen,

This chinchilla's housing, located not far from a window, receives the right amount of light. Place the chinchilla cage in quiet area of the house, with indirect lighting.

family room, or playroom with lots of daily activities is not a good choice; a study or bedroom may work well.

The Right Light

Chinchillas need about twelve hours of light and twelve hours of dark a day; the exact proportion should be similar from day to day, but it can vary from season to season. For example, you shouldn't provide twelve hours light–twelve dark one day and ten light–fourteen dark the next; however, a gradual change with the seasons, so that there is less light in the winter and more in the summer, is fine. An easy way to shift with the seasons is to house the chinchillas in a room with windows that are not shaded. Expose the chinchilla cage to indirect, not direct, sunlight, and make sure it receives the sun's light but not its heat.

Although the chinchillas need light in the day, they should also have a nest box to retreat to, away from the bright light. Take note, too, of the ledge on which the chinchillas roost to sleep, and consider covering the cage on that side to provide a darker area—a cave of sorts—to give your chins a sense of security (do not use cloth to cover the cage, as the fibers, if eaten, could cause internal damage; a collapsed large cardboard moving box, the type without strings or fibers, works well for an inexpensive partial cage cover.)

In very moderate weather, such as a nice spring or fall day in New England or a winter's afternoon in the Deep South, the chinchillas may enjoy having the cage moved near an open window, where they can bask in direct sunlight in temperatures of 60 to 70 degrees Fahrenheit. Make sure the chinchillas can retreat into a nest box or shaded area of the cage to escape the sunlight if they so desire.

Lighting: Imitating Nature

For chinchilla owners who want a more elaborate lighting environment for their pets, forty-year chinchilla veteran Alice Kline recommends simulating a natural outdoor lighting condition as follows: use either a 20-watt Vita-Lite Full Spectrum lamp (available at pet stores or online and sold for birds and reptiles) on a fixture mounted directly above the cage or a 40-watt lamp mounted 4 feet above it. Again, make sure the chinchillas have a nest box for shade and security, just as you would if you were providing natural indirect sunlight.

Temperature

As noted in chapter 2, the temperature in the chinchilla room should never exceed 79 degrees Fahrenheit and should be maintained at temperatures in the range of the mid-60s to low 70s, at most. Chinchillas do not deal well with humidity, either, and do best in a cool, dry location.

Make sure to have both a thermometer and humidistat in the room that your chins are in. During heat waves, check the temperature and humidity reading several times a day if you don't have air-conditioning. A chinchilla needs 30 to 40 percent humidity; anything lower will dry out the fur and cause other health issues, and higher humidity could lead to heatstroke. Add the heat and humidity numbers together to get an HH reading : for example, a temperature of 90 degrees Fahrenheit plus a humidity of 60 percent gives an HH reading of 150. Heat and humidity registering 150 HH or higher can be fatal to chinchillas.

The gold standard in the summer is a room air conditioner because it reduces both temperature and humidity. Even then, you have to take precautions in case you experience power outages or appliance failure. In these cases, do anything you can to keep your chins cool (and dry). Just make sure, whether using an air conditioner, a dehumidifier, or a fan, not to let the air blow directly on the chinchillas. Here are a few tips:

- Buy or borrow a room air conditioner.
- Move the cage to the coolest part of the house, such as the basement.
- Use a dehumidifier.
- Use room-darkening shades to keep the sun out, and dim the lights.
- Put marble tiles that have been cooled in the freezer into the cage for your chinnies to lie on. Tiles designed specifically for this purpose are sold in pet stores; you can also buy tiles cheaply as overstocks from tile stores or even from a large hardware or home-improvement store. (Have several, so you can swap them between cage and freezer every couple of hours). You might even try putting the cage on top of a large, cold marble slab.
- Place water frozen in glass jars into the cage (fill the jars only three-quarters full before freezing!).
- Buy some freezer ice packs, and either put them in a metal box inside the cage or place them around the cage alongside the pullout tray on very hot days. (Do not place them in the cage or against the wire because the chins will chew the plastic and get sick.)
- Put a dish with ice on it in the chinchillas' cage. Don't worry about the chins' eating ice. It won't hurt their teeth.
- Put a fan in the room. For chins, however, a fan is only part of the solution. Fans make us cooler because the rushing air evaporates sweat on our skin, whereas chins cool down by a radiant process; they need the air from the fan to be cooled for it to be effective. Try putting a bundle of wet

towels or sheets near one corner of the cage and directing a fan so it blows on the bundle. Make sure the air hits only the towels, not the chinchillas.

- Put your chins in their travel cage, and take them for an air-conditioned car ride. Consider taking them to a cooler place, such as a friend's house that is air-conditioned or has a finished basement.

Have several of these strategies at the ready for high-heat, high-humidity days, and your chins will stay cool and happy.

A chinchilla beats the heat by sitting on a cooled tile.

Elevation

The chinchilla cage should be placed on a stand or on a sturdy piece of furniture, not directly on the ground where it would be susceptible to temperature fluctuations and drafts. Another reason to keep chinchillas up off the ground is that they want to be at eye level with you. They feel vulnerable having people tower above them (if the cage is low, make sure to sit on the floor when you talk with or take out your chinchillas). Finally, there is a definite advantage to placing a cage on a fitted stand, rather than on the floor or furniture. A stand holds the cage securely when the chinchillas leap between ledges; this reduces the amount the cage shakes (better for them) and the amount of associated noise (better for you).

Home Is Where the Cage Is

Housing for a chinchilla must be designed for the animal's specific needs. Otherwise, broken limbs or other injury may result. Sadly, many pet chinchillas are housed in glass aquariums, which are not appropriate homes for chinchillas. Aquariums do not provide the proper ventilation and could overheat the animals. You cannot easily build ledges inside them, and even if you could, a chinchilla leaping between ledges at high speeds could end up smacking into the glass. The best housing for your chinchillas is a roomy wire cage, elevated off the ground and fitted with replaceable wooden ledges for the chinchillas to leap to and from.

Requirements for Cage Construction

Other than the replaceable wooden ledges, the entire cage should be made of metal. Wooden cages are impossible to completely disinfect, and wet wood takes a long time to dry and may

Well equipped with ledges, toys, a nest box, and a wheel, this large cage provides the space and stimulation a chinchilla needs.

cause your chinchillas to get a chill. To avoid injury, it is very important that the floor and any levels are made of solid materials and not wire.

The dimensions of the cage should be at least 30 inches long, 18 inches deep, and 30 inches high—with chinchilla cages, the bigger the better, up to 4 feet high or so. Some chinchilla lovers even create a permanent play area by fencing off a closet or a corner of the room with a very high dog pen. Chinchillas are amazing leapers, so an open pen would have to be 6 feet or even higher—all the way to the ceiling—to keep a chinchilla inside.

The wire used for the cage should be galvanized or powder-coated to prevent the cage from rusting and from cutting the animal. New cages should be washed in vinegar and rinsed, as the zinc that was used in galvanizing the cage can make a chinchilla sick.

For a cage housing full-grown adult chinchillas, the size of the holes in the wire mesh for the sides of the cage needs to be 1 inch by 2 inches or less. Use 1-inch-by-1/2-inch mesh for cage sides if you have baby chinchillas, are breeding chinchillas, or have a chinchilla that might be pregnant. The smaller spacing on the wire is important so that newborns don't get stuck or crawl through.

Many large cages come with wire ramps, which will need to be removed from the chinchilla cage. Ramps are the number one cause of broken legs in chinchillas, with wire levels or flooring coming in a close second. Use wooden shelves to make ledges for the chinchillas to leap from level to level (which they do with ease). Wood is solid, so it's easy on the animals' legs and feet. Ledges should be staggered on opposite or adjacent sides of the cage at about 12-inch intervals. A tall cage without ledges is simply wasted space.

Other benefits of using wood for the ledges are that the chinchillas can gnaw on the sides of wooden ledges to keep their teeth trim and that wood can easily be replaced if it gets too worn or stained (although chinchillas usually will not pee on their ledges, as long as you don't place one beneath the other).

Make sure the cage bottom is a slide-out tray, both for easy cleaning and for minimally disturbing the chinchillas when you spot clean. A deep pan 4 to 6 inches in height is ideal for keeping a nice deep layer of litter contained in the cage and for reducing the problem of chinchilla poops being expelled out of the cage. (A hand-held vacuum for cleaning up droppings is a good investment, all the same). The floor of the cage should be solid metal, covered by at least two inches of safe litter, such as processed paper, aspen, or kiln-dried pine. Cedar or non-kiln-dried pine (check the package) can cause respiratory or liver problems.

Although I wouldn't recommend it, if you decide to use a raised wire floor with a metal slide-out tray below it, bear in mind that the wire mesh used for flooring must have holes no bigger than ½ by ½ inch to avoid causing a broken leg. Wire mesh is not comfortable on the feet, so make sure the chinchillas have a wooden nest box and wooden ledges to rest on. Some pet owners find that chinchillas that are used to solid-bottom cages go through an adjustment period before they will walk on the wire. Some chinchillas never fully adjust and can suffer a negative personality change.

You can also find specialty or custom-made cages online and in some specialty stores. When purchasing a cage online or from one of these stores, use the specifications outlined in the box to explain your requirements. Quality Cage Company is one online supplier that ships ready-made, chinchilla-appropriate cages that meet these specifications (http://www.qualitycage

Specifications for a Chinchilla Cage

Cage dimensions: At least 30" long x 18" deep x 30" high, and bigger is better
Size of wire mesh for cage sides: Between 1" x 1" and 1" x 2" for adults; 1" x ½" for babies
Cage material: Galvanized or powder-coated metal
Floor material: Solid metal; 3 ½" (or higher) slide-out tray
Ledges material: Replaceable wood

.com/chinchilla.html). Here are a few other suppliers offering cages that could be appropriately modified for chinchillas (for example, by removing wire ramps):

Custom Cage Works
(http://www.cageworks.com/cage_gallery/chin/index.html)

Martin's Cages
(http://www.martinscages.com/products/cages/chinchilla/)

Klubertanz Equipment Company (http://www.klubertanz.com/)

Cage Care

Chinchillas are practically odorless, and the same can be said of their caging. Don't wait for the cage to smell bad before cleaning—it would take quite a while. Instead, for the sake of your chinchillas' health, clean out the cage once a week. Throw away the old litter. Clean the flooring of the cage with a cleaning solution, and rinse well with very hot water. Vacuum the hair off the bars. Check the wooden ledges for soiling; chins usually won't pee on these, but if they do, or if the wood is soiled by soft droppings, spray the area with vinegar and water, scrub it, and let it air dry. You can also sand down the shelving to remove stains and keep it hygienic. About every six months to a year, you'll need to replace the wooden shelves because your chinchillas will gnaw them (this is a good thing!)

There are many safe cleaning solutions available. The simplest is cider vinegar and water. This solution removes residue and doesn't need as thorough a rinsing as bleach does. A little bleach diluted in hot water is another possibility. It can be mixed with an organic or nontoxic biodegradable cleaning product (Simple Green, for example) for added cleaning power. Your veterinarian may recommend or sell other cleaners to sterilize the cage. Stay away from dish soap or similar cleaners that leave a residue that your chinchillas may lick.

The shelving used for ledges can easily be replaced; most hardware stores sell kiln-dried pine and will cut it to your specifications. Fasten the shelves with oversized washers and screws. You can also buy ledges and hardware for chinchillas at pet stores, although the ledges are generally smaller. Definitely replace the ledges when the wood is gnawed down close to the screws and before these are exposed; chipping a tooth on the metal would be bad news.

The water bottle and bowls can be cleaned with vinegar and water or bleach and water, or you can run them through the dishwasher. Toys such as metal wheels and saucers should be wiped down or washed during the weekly cleaning.

A few times a year, take the whole cage outside and clean it, sidings and all, with bleach and water. Hose it down and leave it out to sun dry.

Cage Accessories

You will need a number of accessories in addition to the cage and ledges: water bottles, food bowls (one for pellets and a smaller one for supplement), chew blocks, a dust-bath house or bowl, a nest box, exercise equipment, and toys. A travel cage is another good investment and has multiple uses. Providing a litter box in the cage is optional.

Litter Box

Because chinchillas tend to pick a favorite corner to urinate in, providing a litter box can be worthwhile. You cannot train chinchillas to use a litter box, but by observing which corners they

A pullout tray, shown here, not only holds a deep layer of litter but also makes cage cleaning a breeze.

urinate in (most likely the back ones) and putting litter boxes there, you can keep the cage cleaner between weekly cleanings. Chinchillas like to use their own corners, so if you have two chinchillas, you will need two litter boxes. Most chinchillas will chew plastic, which can be fatal if ingested, so the litter box or pan should be made of metal; an alternative is to use the disposable heavy cardboard kind. You can fill it with a type of small animal cage litter that has the appearance and consistency of kitty litter but is made of paper. Because the urine is not very pungent, a litter box is not really necessary, and you may not want to take up the room with the corner boxes, especially if your cage is small. Instead, use a thick layer of aspen bedding, shake a little baking soda in the favorite peeing spots, and replace the litter in those corners between cleanings, if necessary.

Food and Water Receptacles

For feeding your chinchilla, use a dome-shaped bowl or heavy crock-type bowl, 4 inches in diameter. It also needs to be tip-resistant, especially if the cage floor is wire. Check and change the food every day. Use a separate ceramic bowl, 2 inches in diameter, to feed any supplemental grains or treats.

Chinchillas must have clean, fresh water at all times. Give it to them in a water bottle, not a bowl, so they don't spill water or get their fur wet. The nozzle should be set at a 45-degree angle. You may have to go online to find and order an ideal chinchilla water bottle. Look for a wide-mouth bottle that can be easily and thoroughly cleaned; you'll need to rinse the water bottle and replace the water every day as well as make washing the water bottle part of your weekly cage-cleaning routine.

Mount the water bottle on the outside of the cage to prevent the chinchillas from gnawing on the hard plastic; a glass water bottle is even better. Outside mounting also allows you to get at the water bottle easily without opening the cage, so your chins will have less opportunity to escape for an unauthorized

This sturdy ceramic bowl full of pellets won't be easily tipped over by a hungry chin.

free-run session. Some people use bottled water or boil tap water (cooling it before use) to prevent any chance that their chins will get internal parasites from the water. If your tap water is treated with a softener and has salt and additives in it, you should give your chins bottled water.

Nest Box

Chinchillas need a nest box to hide in and sleep in. You can purchase one made of untreated white pine or build one yourself, if you are handy. Make sure the dimensions allow your chinchilla to stand comfortably on all fours and turn around. If you have two chinchillas, both should be able to fit comfortably in the box without pressing against one another (although they are likely to want to cuddle on cooler days). The nest box should have an open back for ventilation, no floor because the chinchillas would urinate on it, and a hole in the front to allow the chins to go in and out and to peer out of the box. Ideally, the box sides and top should be assembled with wooden dowels rather than with metal nails or screws, so the chins can safely gnaw on the wood.

Chew Block

Chins need and love to chew wood, and it keeps their teeth trim and healthy. That is one reason for providing wooden ledges and nest boxes. In addition, give your chinchillas a clean block of untreated pine meant specifically for gnawing. Chins also like to hold, carry, and chew on small wooden discs.

Dust and Dust-Bath Bowl

Chinchillas need to take a dry bath in chinchilla dust at least a few times a week, or even every day, to keep them well groomed

A chinchilla enjoys a dust bath while another waits her turn. Dust baths are so popular, it's not surprising that there's a line to get in!

and in good health. (Chinchillas shouldn't get wet; see the section on grooming in chapter 5 for more on this.) Dust baths are a favorite playtime activity, too. Most pet stores sell chinchilla dust; online chinchilla specialty stores carry the highest quality dust—the kind used for show chinchillas—and sell it in bulk. Pet stores sell dust-bath houses designed specifically for chinchillas, completely enclosed except for an entry hole and available in plastic or ceramic. A large, half-covered small animal ceramic bowl works well, too. In a pinch, any small plastic bin will work, although the dust will fly during the chinchilla's exuberant roll. Make sure not to leave a plastic dust-bath house (or anything else plastic) in the cage; you don't want the chinchillas to gnaw and possibly ingest the plastic.

Toys

Chinchillas have active minds, dexterous paws, and teeth built for gnawing. Add to the mix fragile bones and a very sensitive digestive tract, and you have a problem: many toys are hazardous to them. Nevertheless, chinchillas are curious animals whose brains and bodies need to be kept occupied. Safe toys kept in the cage (and other toys used only with supervision) can be a partial solution. Providing a stimulating cage with levels and ledges (but no ramps and no wire flooring, please!) as well as a chinchilla friend (whether or not housed in the same cage), time with you, free runs, and music or family-programming television at night adds other important stimulation to ensure that your chinchillas are happy and healthy.

Toys for Inside the Cage

Don't assume that an item is safe just because there is a picture of a chinchilla on the packaging. Many manufacturers are primarily interested in profit; others just don't understand how creative chinchillas are at using toys in ways other than intended. Make sure that the toy cannot be eaten and that it cannot choke or hang a chinchilla or allow her to get a paw or leg caught in it. Some safe toys are: little pieces of pine wood in varying sizes and shapes (chinchillas especially like circles that are 2 to 2½ inches in diameter); sticks or climbing branches of apple tree wood (or other safe fruit tree wood); and large, sturdy cardboard tubes to run through, roll, and gnaw.

Many chinchillas appreciate a cuttlebone or pumice stone to gnaw, in addition to wooden toys; these materials also help keep the animals' constantly growing teeth trim. Grass mats and Roll-A-Nest hay balls with openings to climb into are huge hits, though quickly demolished. One caution: these toys are held together by wire, and if you ever see any of the wire exposed, the toy needs to be removed and thrown away. You can purchase these and other fun chin toys online at http://www.chinworld.com. Linked "log" toys are also fun for chinchillas, and they can be transformed into new toys depending on how you bend them.

Solid metal wheels and saucers are expensive toys, but chins enjoy them immensely. Do not use a plastic wheel; even hard plastic is ingestible, and the way the wheel attaches to the cage can cause injury. The worst wheels are those with a bar in the middle. Chinchillas don't run in the wheel the way a typical pet rodent—say, a hamster or a rat—does. Instead, they leap-run and will rub fur and bang their backs on the bar.

Chinchillas love a hiding house to play in or take refuge in. The wooden nest box described earlier does double duty as a hiding house. Another possibility is a large terra-cotta garden pot. Knock out the bottom so it doesn't get soiled with droppings and urine. An added benefit to this toy is that it can be chilled in the freezer and used to cool the chins' environment during a heat wave or if your air-conditioning fails. You might want to get two so that you can alternate putting one in the freezer and one in the cage every hour or two until the temperature goes down.

Toys for Supervised Play

Chinchillas love a hanging bird toy, but the issue is what to hang it with. Rope or string with indigestible fiber is out! Wires can also be dangerous if they are flexible and can wrap around a chinchilla. Chains work, provided the chin can't get a paw stuck in the link; one possibility is a tight-linked dog choke, or training, collar. Or just use a clip or ring to hang the toy to the cage top or side. A special ingestible rope called sisal is on the market for hanging chinchilla toys. If the chinchillas do gnaw it extensively,

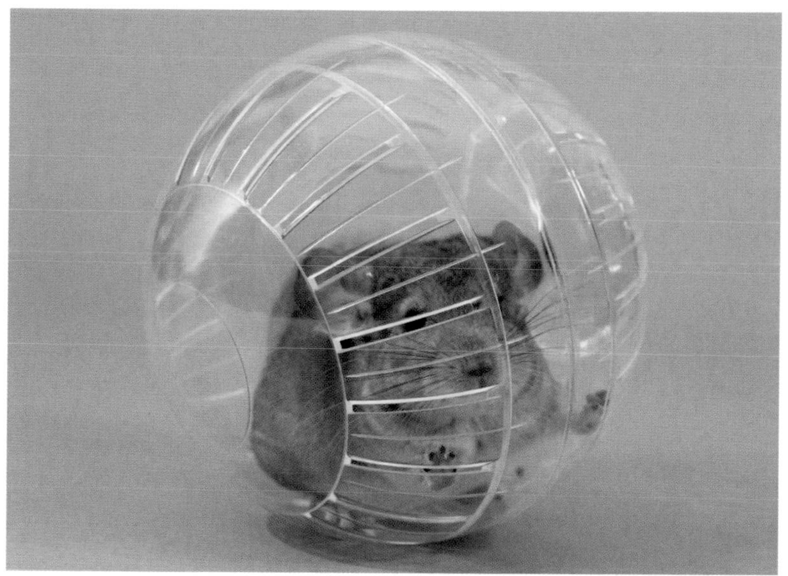

This chinchilla runs in an exercise ball. Before letting a chinchilla run wild in a run-around ball, make sure it is a cool day and that she is constantly supervised to avoid any chance of overheating.

you should probably change to chain. Any frayed rope can get wrapped around little paws, and even if it is digestible as advertised, sisal is not on the approved chinchilla diet!

You can use chain to hang a PVC pipe and make a hanging tunnel. Even though PVC is plastic, it is such thick plastic that many chinchillas don't gnaw on it. If yours do, remove the toy immediately from the cage and make it a supervised playtime toy.

If you offer wooden hanging toys, as with other wooden toys, stick to the hard woods: kiln-dried pine and fruit tree woods (apple, pear, or mulberry, for example). Steer clear of tongue depressors or other thin, soft wooden items that can splinter. Visit http://www.pet-chinchilla-toys.com: this is a fun site for chin hanging toys or components for putting together your own. All the toys use sisal rope, and the site offers sisal separately, too.

The use of giant run-around balls that chinchillas run inside of is somewhat controversial in chinchilla circles. Some swear by them, and others think they are too dangerous. This toy definitely falls into the supervised play category. Run-around balls are nice when free runs aren't feasible or before your chinchilla is fully tamed. If you have two chinchillas, either have them take turns or get them each a ball; they can't work the same ball in tandem, and it will also create too much body heat to have two animals in one ball. Run-around balls should be used only in temperatures lower than 70 degrees Fahrenheit, or your chinchilla will overheat; this is not a toy for a hot summer day! Set a timer, and check on your chinchilla every fifteen minutes. If the animal's fur looks greasy and ratty, rather than dry and soft, it is too hot in there, and it's time to end the run. During the check, empty out any poops. The chinchilla probably won't pee in the ball, but should it happen, immediately take your pet out and wash the exercise ball thoroughly.

If budget and space allow, set up a 4- to 6-foot-high pen around the cage for supervised playtimes. Teach your chins that they may not climb over and play outside the pen by telling them "no" if they try and by ending the playtime if they ignore your admonitions.

Homemade Playthings

You can make toys, too. Chinchillas love an empty cellophane or aluminum foil roll (no glue!); cut it lengthwise so they won't get a head stuck inside. Mine also like to hold, carry, and gnaw on "business cards" made from index cards. Here's another idea: Create a chinchilla play place by putting fun items inside a taped-up, medium-size U-Haul box in which you've cut a small entry hole.

Put old papers, smaller boxes of various sizes, and crumpled brown paper bags inside. One or more peepholes and a back entrance are optional. Put several of these boxes on shelves for chinchillas to pop in and out of, creating an elaborate simulated mountainside play space.

Travel Cage

Finally, another very practical investment is a travel cage. It should be just big enough for two chinchillas to fit comfortably inside without having to touch each other and with room enough to turn around and stand up on their hind legs. When traveling with your pets, transfer them to the travel cage; it will take up less space in the car, and your chinchillas won't have room in which to leap around if they get startled or upset during the drive. You can collapse their main home, pack it in the trunk, and set it up when you arrive at your final destination. Furryflowers.com sells a well-designed travel cage with single or multiple units (http://furryflowers.com).

There are other uses for a small cage, too. It is hoped this will never occur, but if your chinchillas ever fight, you will need to separate them, and a travel cage can be temporary housing for one. A travel cage can be used during weekly cage cleaning as well, if you can't give your chins a free run during this time. It also gives you an easy way to transport your pets to the veterinarian for an office visit.

You may want to leave the travel cage near the main cage and let your chins play in and on it during free runs. You can also give them their dust bath (see chapter 5) in the travel cage. This way, when you use the travel cage, it will already be a familiar home away from home.

CHAPTER

4

Welcoming and Taming the New Arrivals

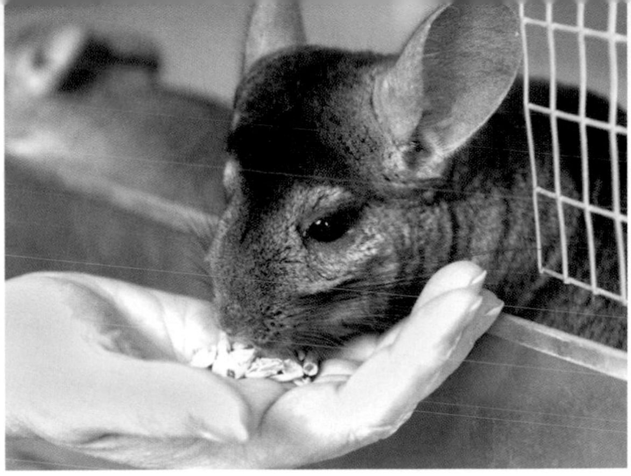

A chinchilla receives the perfect housewarming gift—a small handful of oats.

THE FIRST FEW DAYS AND WEEKS AFTER BRINGING YOUR CHINchillas home are an important time in their development and in building your relationship with them. They may travel and adjust a little better if you bring them home early in the day, when they are sleepy. Schedule their arrival for a week when you have some time available to dedicate to them.

Veterinary Visit

In addition to setting up the cage and its accessories, you'll need to attend to the chins' diet and make arrangements for a veterinarian in advance. Be prepared at first to feed the brand of food that your chinchilla is accustomed to eating. If you want to switch brands, purchase a two-month supply of the current food type from the breeder or a pet store. For the first two weeks, use the current food exclusively. Then, mix in just a little of the new food with it, and increase the percentage of the new food a little bit every couple of days. After several weeks, you will have switched over completely to the new brand.

It is always a good idea to set up an initial well-visit appointment with a veterinarian one week after your chinchillas are settled in their new home. Continue to bring your pets to the veterinarian for annual checkups. Make sure the doctor is an expert in chinchilla health, illness, and injury. You may be able to see the same doctor your breeder uses, or you can get a recommendation from other local chinchilla owners. The veterinarian will verify gender; check the chinchilla's teeth, temperature, and heart (making sure there is no heart murmur); and check stools for worms.

Welcome Home

Bring your new chinchillas home in a small secure box or covered travel cage, and move them directly into their new home. The one exception is for ranch chinchillas or those raised in similar small quarters. For these animals, a sudden change—not only to a completely new environment and unfamiliar caregivers but also to a spacious, open cage—may send them into a panic. They will need to be transitioned slowly from the travel cage to their new housing over several days. (See pages 77–78 for more on bringing home ranch chinchillas.)

When picking up your chinchillas from their current home, make sure they don't get chilled; warm up the car and cover the cage with a blanket if it is cold outside. Plan to drive straight home to minimize the stress of the trip. Once home, if

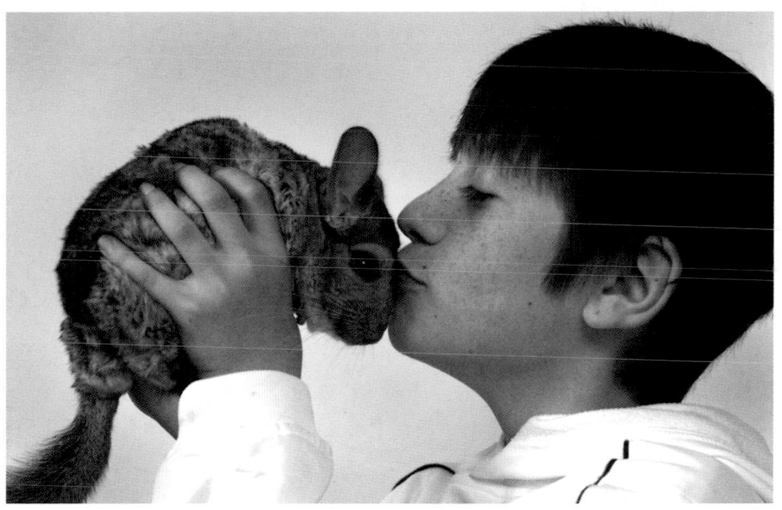

The affectionate bond between this boy and his pet chinchilla is very apparent.

you have any difficulty retrieving the chins from the carrier cage and getting them into their home, there's no need to rush the process. You can leave them in the carrier with food and water for a few hours or place the opened carrier inside the new cage and let them emerge when they are ready. After placing the chinchillas in their cage, leave them undisturbed for the day (make sure they have a roomy nest box to hide and sleep in).

Chinchillas depend on their routine for security, and they will probably be overwhelmed and frightened at first. Resist the urge to invite friends and family over to see the new additions to the family. Even completely tamed and adjusted chinchillas often are not keen on strangers, and at this time, having new people peering into the cage and chattering excitedly would be especially stressful. It can be difficult for children in the home to understand and respect the chinchillas' need for some alone and quiet time. Perhaps you can take pictures of the chinchillas at the breeders for the children to look at and to show off to others.

Don't Rush the Introduction

The first evening the animals are home, very quietly approach the cage and speak softly to your chinchillas. Do they retreat into the nest box? Do they remain perched on the ledge but pressed up against the back corner? If so, move to a spot several feet away, and engage in a quiet activity, such as reading, paying bills, knitting, or watching television. Dim the lights a bit so the chinchillas can get a better look at you. (Their vision in bright light is poor and improves in low light conditions.) Let them get used to how you look, smell, move, and sound.

If your chinchillas seem confident and curious, coming to the front of the cage and pressing their noses through the bars, then sit right next to the cage. Spend about a half hour talking to them, and start making friends. When getting to know your chinchillas, take your time. Do not rush things. It is best if they are introduced first to a single adult who will be their primary caretaker. Once they come to know and trust this individual, they will be ready to meet other people and pets in the household.

Handling the New Arrivals

Do not let your chinchillas out of their cage too soon. They should stay in the cage for the first few days to a week. Then, bring them out one at a time; make sure they stay in your arms every time you take them out for the next two weeks. Hold them for a few minutes a session, totaling about twenty minutes of out-of-cage time a day. Then, allow them to explore a limited space, such as a covered tabletop, for the following two weeks. At that point, you can try letting them run in a small, confined, chinchilla-proofed space, such as the bathroom—after it has been thoroughly scrubbed with a nontoxic cleaner.

Adjusting Ranch Chinchillas to Home Life

The standards for chinchilla ranches require that animals be housed in at least 2,200 cubic inches of space (about 12 x 12 ½ x 14 inches), and the animals are usually housed individually. A chinchilla raised singly in a small cage becomes accustomed to this setup and the limited mobility it affords. The cage enveloping the animal becomes a sort of security blanket. A 30 x 18 x 30 inch cage, which I recommend as the minimum size housing for pet chinchillas, affords more than seven times the space! So for a ranch-bred animal, the move to a new, spacious cage takes a huge adjustment. To ease the transition, provide a starter cage similar in dimensions to the one the chin is accustomed to, and allow time for him to make a gradual transition from this cage into the larger one. Otherwise, your little newcomer may go into a panicked frenzy of activity and could die of related stress and exhaustion.

The stress of travel and a new environment may bring on constipation. Feed two raisins a day (for constipation) for the first week; give one raisin a day for the second week. Continue with one raison every other day until the transition period is completed. The chinchilla may need to get used to the texture of a raisin at first, so just leave the raisin in the food bowl if your pet won't take it from your hand right away. Find out if the rancher used any form of ambient noise (such as a radio playing), and reproduce that aspect of the old environment.

It is important that all chinchillas eat the food they have been used to eating when coming into a new home. For a ranch chinchilla whose world has been rocked, it is critical. Make sure the chinchilla is drinking, too, by carefully monitoring how much water disappears from the bottle. Chins in the ranch may have had an automatic water dispenser with a pin they needed to hit to let out the liquid. Licking at the water bottle tube is likely to be a new concept. If the chin is not drinking, try offering water through a syringe or adding some natural cranberry or apple juice (no added sugar) to the water in the water bottle and tapping it to bring a drop of juice to the bottom; that should encourage the chin to start licking at it.

Once the chinchilla is eating, drinking, and becoming friendly toward you, you can make the transition into a larger cage and then introduce another chinchilla. Having been raised in close quarters with other chinchillas may make a ranch chinchilla receptive to sharing a cage with a chinchilla friend.

Introducing Chinchillas to One Another

By far the best and easiest thing to do is to bring home two chinchillas that are already together and fast friends: two young males, two females, a mother and daughter, or a father and son. Next best would be to introduce two babies that are about ten weeks old. With babies, a direct introduction is possible, which means putting both into a freshly cleaned cage. They should get along fine.

With adults, be aware that the personality of the chinchilla is likely to change with the introduction of a new friend. A touchy female may become more chilled out, and a passive male more outgoing and energetic; a chinchilla that couldn't get enough playtime with you before may be more interested in "staying home with the wife and kids."

Adult introductions are possible, but there are no guarantees. If you have an older lone chinchilla (especially a male) that is active and outgoing, you may want to leave him as is. Make

Chinchillas that are well acquainted can temporarily share a split cage, as shown. Chinchillas that are strangers must be introduced to each other gradually and carefully in separate cages.

sure he has a roomy cage, toys, lots of exploring time, and extra attention from you. If you think he needs some company of his own kind, you could try a one-on-one introduction. Even if the pair don't work out as cage mates, they will probably enjoy very much being neighbors.

Typically, the easiest adult introduction is a male-female pairing. Assuming you don't want thirty or more chinchillas in addition to these two, the male should be neutered. This can be a delicate operation and one pursued only under the recommendation of a veterinarian experienced in successfully neutering chinchillas (see the box entitled "Neutering" in chapter 2). Or adopt a chinchilla that is already neutered from an animal shelter or rescue; many of them are. The next easiest introduction is a female-female pairing—either two adults, or one adult and a ten-week-old. Males can be paired if both are no older than four months. When pairing male youngsters, you may find that nonsiblings sometimes get along better than two that were raised together. Brothers sometimes get into the habit almost from birth of pushing and shoving for food and for mom's attention and can bring those behaviors into their adult lives.

When matching chinchillas, find two that have similar dominant and submissive traits. An overly dominant chinchilla can wear down a cage mate over time. Two chinchillas that are even-tempered, neither one markedly aggressive nor subdued, are good candidates for an introduction.

One common method of introducing adult chinchillas is to place them in separate cages located side by side. Leave about six inches of space between the cages—this represents the No Bite zone. Even if both shove paws or noses through the wires, they cannot get at each other. Every few days, swap the chinchillas between cages so that they start to learn each other's scent. Do not let them play together or otherwise come in direct contact during this stage of the introduction. After a few weeks and when the chinchillas seem to be interested in but not aggressive toward each other, move the more dominant of the two into the more submissive one's cage (this way, the dominant one will not feel the need to be territorial), or put them together in a freshly clean (neutral) cage.

Make the introduction in the daytime, when the chins are less active, and on a day when you are home. Watch the pair carefully for the first day. If the chinchillas fight or you see bite marks on the ears, face, or back of the neck, the introduction is not working out. The two must be separated immediately and go into their individual cages for a while; give them several more weeks of cage swapping before trying them together again.

It also should be said that relationships can unravel, even for chinchillas that were raised together or were successfully introduced and have lived together for some time. These are intelligent animals with unique and distinctive personalities. A case of irreconcilable differences can occur. Even if the two are not compatible enough to live in the same cage, being herd animals, they are likely to enjoy the company of a neighbor in a nearby cage. They may still be able to share a neutral play area, but only under constant and close supervision.

When animals are caged side by side for companionship, either as singles or in pairs, they should be of the same gender—all girls, all boys, or all breeding pairs—to prevent any hormonally induced tension or squabbling. Chinchillas housed together (or even side by side) tend to be more active and more vocal than lone chinchillas. Having others of their kind to interact and communicate with can give them a "safety in numbers" feeling of security.

Introducing Your Chinchilla to Other Animals

In the first few weeks after the chinchillas' homecoming, keep any other household pets in a separate area of the house. Once the chinchillas are comfortable in their new home and are well on their way to making friends with you, other animals can be introduced under a careful eye. Many dogs will get quite excited and worked up about having chinchillas in the home; imagine their surprise and delight when they discover you've captured two live, fat squirrels for them! Both the smell and the movement are intoxicating to dogs with any hunting instinct whatsoever.

Make it clear to your dog that the chinchillas are for viewing only and not to be touched. A dog that cannot resist poking a nose through the cage should immediately be told "No!" and removed from the room. Repeat this until the dog gets the message. Even though canines are natural predators, chinchillas will come to relax in the presence of a dog taught to respect the chinchillas' boundaries. Never let the chinchillas run loose in a room with a dog present. Chinchillas on the loose have a way of arousing a dormant hunt instinct in even the most unlikely of doggie predators.

The chinchilla's size alone may deter a cat from stalking or preying on them. However, a large or avid hunting cat may think otherwise. Do not let cats and chinchillas play together or even stay in the same room unsupervised (as sharp claws may find their way into the cage).

This dog is curious about his new furry housemate. Despite their natural hunting instinct, dogs must learn the rule "paws off."

Separate the Pets

SIMPLY PUT, CHINCHILLAS CANNOT PLAY WITH ANY OTHER household pets.

- ***Make the immediate area around the chinchilla cage a No Pet Trespassing zone.***
- ***Ensure that any pets that have claws, paws, noses, or heads that can fit into the chinchilla cage never run loose and unsupervised around the cage.***

Ferrets and rats, though smaller than cats and dogs, are also predatory animals and can agitate, chase, or injure chinchillas (which are prey animals). Ferrets and rats must not be allowed to commune with the chinchillas or climb on their cages. Even the pint-size gerbil, whose Latin name means "clawed warrior," can pursue or terrorize a timid chinchilla if playtimes overlap.

Taming the Woolly Chinchilla

To tame your chinchillas, do not give them too much free rein too soon. Start by getting to know them, first with the chinchillas in the cage, then in your arms, and then running in a confined space. You want to avoid the situation of having to chase and capture a frightened chinchilla. To begin taming the animals, wait until they show interest in you and start begging to come out, usually in the early morning or early evening, when they are awake but not too hyped up. Until then, even if it takes days or weeks, sit next to the cage while engaged in another activity or just talk to them and hand-feed them; pick out the oats from the supplement, and hand-feed these through the cage.

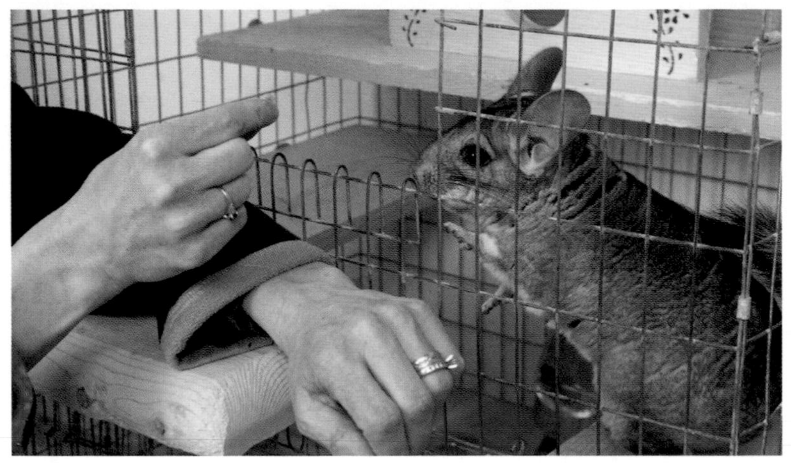

Using a treat, a chinchilla owner entices her pet out of the cage and onto her arm.

Put your face up close to the bars and let the chinchillas sniff or rub noses with you. If they wink at you, they are saying, "Hi, there!"—so wink back. Rest your arm in the cage, holding it perfectly still with some oats on your hand, and let the chins explore you. You can cut a raisin in four and feed one piece at a time for a very special reward when they are making progress in becoming tame.

You may find after a few days that your chinchillas (especially baby chins) are nibbling on you. This is a good sign. It is exploratory behavior, especially common in babies who are still in the putting-everything-in-the-mouth stage. It is a sign that they are getting to know you and are getting comfortable with you. Even older chinchillas can get into the habit of grooming you as though you were another chinchilla; consider this the highest honor! If the nibbling is ever hard enough to be uncomfortable or hurt you, let your pets know in terms they understand: don't jerk your hand away, but instead, give a squeak or say "Ouch!" They should get the message.

To pet your chinchillas, keep your hand within their line of sight, where they can see it. Many like to be rubbed on the chest or stroked on the side of the nose, under the chin, or around the front legs. Very few like to be petted on the back.

Once the chinchillas will come out of an open cage door into your arms, hold them for ten to fifteen minutes at a time. If after a few weeks the chinchillas are still not coming to you, you can either give them more time or try to pick them up. If they leap madly around the cage, blow fur, or show other signs of distress when you try to pick them up, they are not ready for this step. In this case, spend more time resting your hands in the cage, letting the chinchillas come to you and hand-feeding them oats. If they are not overly concerned with your placing two hands in the cage, however, let them settle down; then, gently but with confidence, herd one into a corner and scoop the animal up and out of the cage in a fast motion. Hold the chin up close against your body for just a few minutes. Make sure to hold on and not drop the animal, despite any squirming. Then put the chinchilla back in the cage and immediately give a treat (a Cheerio or half a raisin). A very softly spoken "Wow!" or "Yeah" or even "Good boy!" or "Good girl!" can enforce how pleased you are with the chin's cooperation and bravery.

Out of Your Arms and onto the Table

An untamed chinchilla allowed to run free can be hard to catch and scared by the chase; the fright can undo all your previous taming work. So don't let the chinchillas down from your arms until they are completely comfortable with you and let you pick them up and hold them without too much struggle, which will probably take about a month. When you first let them down from your arms, do so in a very small and confined space. Try doing so for the first time in the early evening, when the chinchillas are just waking up. A card table or kitchen table works well to give them the first taste of freedom while you remain in control. (Given the poop factor, plan to cover the table with a small tarp or plastic tablecloth bought expressly for this purpose.) Make sure the table is within a larger chinchilla-proofed area. Close all doors to the room and have all hiding spots blocked off.

It may be easier if you work with one chinchilla at a time, especially if you are alone. Try to recruit a second person (someone the chinchilla knows and likes) to sit, without speaking, at the other end of the table to prevent any escape. If the chinchilla looks ready to jump off the table, firmly say "No!" If it does happen, there will be a moment in which the animal freezes after hitting the floor; be prepared to scoop your pet up quickly before the next take-off. If there are a few more escape attempts, directly and without comment put the chinchilla back in the cage for the evening.

Down from the Table and Feet on the Ground

When you do give your chinchillas their first free run, start with a limited space such as a thoroughly cleaned bathroom (close the toilet seat!) with no hiding places. When playtime is over and you want to put your chins back in their cage, slowly follow, corner, and catch them, speaking softly all the while. Do not chase. There are many ways to recapture chinchillas besides picking them up: you can herd them into the cage or a penned-off area or make a tempting transporter (for example, a wide-diameter tube with a closed end or an enclosed box that has a small entry hole and an inviting layer of chinchilla dust inside).

Never chase your chinchillas; they scare easily and have very long memories. Move slowly, being careful not to frighten them. Teach them a special word for what you want, such as *home*, and teach them that going home means fresh food, Cheerios (or some other treat), supplement time, hay, and a dust bath. Eventually, once you start into herding mode and say "Home," they may jump right into the cage in anticipation.

If, after their first free run in the bathroom, they panic when you try to catch them, you may have moved through the taming steps too quickly. Start over again, working through the process; move back to the card table stage, or even earlier, and proceed through the steps more slowly this time.

Once the chinchillas will let you pick them up or willingly go back into the cage with a little herding in the right direction, then begin to increase the size of the free-run area.

Taming Problems

Your chinchilla may seem panicked at being picked up and held, even after several weeks of taming. Your first step is to assess the situation. Is the problem the chinchilla? Is it your handling (too rough, too forward, too rushed, too tentative)? Or is it a combination of the two? You may want to spend some time working one on one with the breeder or with another chinchilla expert—in person is best—to figure out what's going on and how to customize the taming process to your special case. Perhaps you need to adjust your expectations of this particular animal. Sometimes the best approach is to let a more timid chinchilla follow the lead of one that is comfortable with you. When one is sitting on your lap eating oat treats or rolling in the dust bath placed just outside the cage door, the other will soon follow.

Another taming approach for the hard cases is "moving the mountain to Mohammad": you may just have to climb into the cage with the chinchillas. The best way to do this is to create a large enclosed area by setting up a pen (4 feet or higher) around the cage. Then, leave the cage door open; even though chinchillas can scramble over a 4-foot pen easily, they normally will behave when you're watching and discouraging such behavior. Visit inside the pen, sitting very still and building up to hours at a time. Work on other things and ignore the chinchillas. They are curious animals and will want to come over and see what you are doing. Over time,

This chinchilla enthusiast has created a cage big enough to fit both her and her chinchilla. Taming is easier when the chin and the owner are in close proximity.

they will become accustomed to your presence. Eventually, you'll probably find them coming to enjoy your company, even sitting in your lap and crawling up on your shoulder. Keeping your hand full of oats during these sessions will help things along.

Free Run of the Place

Chinchillas absolutely love free run times, when they can take off at top speed and leap from object to object. They should be watched carefully as they roam free, though, because they get into everything and may gnaw something harmful to them or important to you. I've discovered that the quieter they are, the naughtier they are, and items that are left out such as that paycheck you need to deposit are mighty tempting! Mine also have developed a taste for wallpaper (or maybe it is just fun to peel it off the wall). In any case, a chinchilla's extended lingering behind the big armchair is suspect; a "Hey! What are you doing back there?" usually flushes out the guilty party.

Chinchilla Proofing

Domestic chinchillas are not famous for their self-preservation abilities. There are countless chinchilla accidents waiting to happen, including drowning, poisoning, electrocution, choking, and broken limbs. Electric wires (which should be inaccessible, covered, or kept up off the ground), medicines, cleaners, chemicals, and houseplants—these are all potential dangers because chinchillas never really outgrow that putting-everything-in-the-mouth stage. In fact, you may observe that at around age two, your chinchillas go through a notable *increase* in the amount and intensity of gnawing, then pretty much stay at that level for the rest of their lives.

Before allowing a free run, chinchilla proof the room, removing every item you don't want gnawed. Block off any small escape routes such as vents into the heating system or access into the walls. Chinchillas are mostly fur and can squeeze into much smaller spaces than one imagines they can. Make sure that any bookshelves or bureaus are blocked off or pressed right up against the walls. You may want to tip up the mattress so they cannot hide under the bed. And during the free run, you'll need to keep an eye on any fixtures your chins become fixated on.

Stay Close By

Stay in the room whenever the chinchillas are out and about, not only because in your absence they will quickly embark on a gnaw-and-destroy mission but also because they like having you around. With chinchillas, quantity time when they can enjoy just having you there is as important as quality time when you devote your full attention to them. They seem to like an audience of one—namely you—as they play. A cute action that gets a chuckle from you is likely to be repeated over and over again.

One popular play option is to use a tall dog pen and put a bunch of playthings in there—ideally you being one of them. A 4- to 6-foot-high pen is sufficient to keep a chinchilla contained, under your watchful eye. When not being supervised, chinchillas need to be in an enclosure with a cover, or they will scale walls that are just about any height.

Chinchilla Hideout

If your chinchilla-proofing attempts fall short and your free-running chin goes into hiding—for example, into a reclining chair or behind heavy furniture—stay calm. If fully tame and

Chin Proofing Basics

***Make sure there are no places for the chinchilla** to hide in or escape through and that the area is free of potential hazards.*

- ***Take dogs and cats out of the room, and cage any other small animals.***
- ***Secure electric cords up off the ground, or cover them with flexible tubing.***
- ***Remove medicines, cleaners, and toxic chemicals, including cigarettes and ashtrays.***
- ***Put away toiletries and other products that are not for tasting—bars of soap, for example.***
- ***Move poisonous houseplants into another room.***
- ***Make sure there is no lead (lead paint, pipes, drapery weights, and so on) accessible.***
- ***Look for any drowning hazards, such as an open toilet, water in the sink, or a bucket of water.***
- ***Make sure that doors are closed and that windows either are closed or have secure screens.***
- ***Hide any tempting plastic, fiber, or rope chewables, as well as your important papers and books.***
- ***Make sure no plastic bags are within reach.***
- ***Turn off or block off space heaters or other heating units that could burn your chinchilla.***

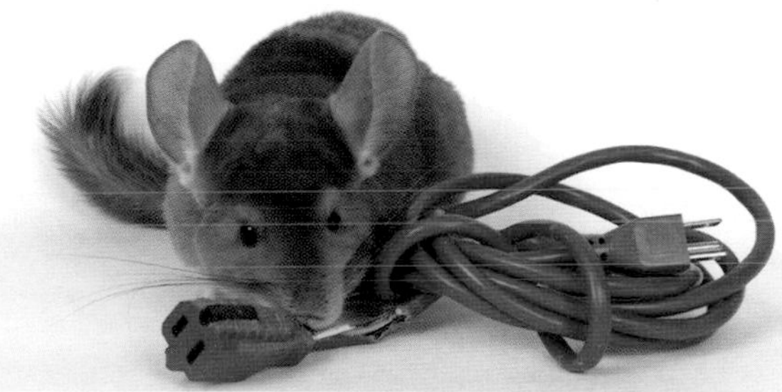

Watch out! A veteran at gnawing, our furry friend is ready to sink his teeth into that extension cord. An unsupervised chinchilla will make fast work of cords and other household hazards.

This chinchilla has wedged himself behind a dresser. Chinchillas can fit into small spaces, so use patience when coaxing them out.

offered a treat or dust bath, the fugitive is likely to come right out. This is why the early stages of taming are so important, as is not rushing to give chinchillas too much freedom too early. When your little escapee does venture out, someone else can slip a barrier in place to prevent the animal heading back for the hiding spot once he is loaded up with treats. Then, focus on herding or catching your pet.

If the chinchilla is not tamed or is enjoying the newfound cave, the attention, and this game immensely, proceed slowly and carefully. The biggest hazard at this point is likely to be your squashing your small pet in a desperate attempt to extract him or her immediately. If you can move or take apart the hiding spot without any possible injury to the chinchilla, then fine. Otherwise, wait out the fugitive. Close the door to the room and chinchilla proof the rest of it. Dim the lights, if you haven't already. Offer incentives to come out—a dust bath, treats or food, water, a tube or box, cage, or cage mate. If you can gently flush out the chin, do so, but do not do anything that is going to scare the animal. It invariably doesn't work; your chin will just hunker down to avoid the mean old world out there. Even if it takes a day or two for your pet to emerge, it will happen eventually, and the chin will be none the worse for the wear. Under your watchful eye, a chin visitor (caged!) of the opposite sex may do the trick, if all else fails. Or in your absence, set a rabbit-size live animal trap loaded with hay and a couple of raisins.

Chinchilla on the Lam

If your chinchilla escapes and you don't know where in the house to look, the first step is to confine dogs and cats to a chinchilla-free bathroom or other area. Close all doors so the chinchilla cannot move from room to room, and remove major hazards such as poisonous houseplants from all rooms. Set up a food, water, and dust bath station in each closed-off room, and watch to see which one gets used; watch also for telltale poop trails. Chinchillas have no problem racing up and down stairs, so search the whole house. They like hiding in closets and in spaces behind bookshelves or other furniture, inside drawers, between the mattress and headboard, or anywhere they can wedge themselves. They hide, then peer out, silently watching you seek. If you have more than one chin living in your household, check and double-check the area where the remaining chin is housed; herd animals tend to not stray too far from their own kind. Once you figure out which room the chinchilla is hiding in, look in every 4-by-4-inch or bigger space during the day while he's sleeping, or sit very quietly in the semidark in the evening and wait for him to come out.

CHAPTER

5

Chinchilla Feeding and Daily Care

A chinchilla feeds on pellets, the staple of the chinchilla diet.

CHINCHILLAS ARE NOT HARD TO FEED, BUT THEY DO HAVE VERY specific dietary needs. It is important to know what foods they can eat and—just as important—what foods are harmful to them. In addition to providing food and water every day, you need to give them frequent dust baths to keep their fur clean, soft, and shiny.

It's Supper Time!

Pet chinchillas are strictly herbivores (hay and grain eaters) with a very delicate digestive tract composed of a stomach and intestines but no gall bladder; they need high fiber and cannot process sugar or much fat. Chinchillas are much like two-year-olds in a candy store when it comes to diet. If it were left up to them, they would gorge themselves on inappropriate treats and quickly eat themselves sick (or even to death). Like a child who craves junk food, a chinchilla that has tasted goodies develops an intense desire for them, especially if treat time is perceived as part of the established routine. (And yes, spoiled chinchillas can throw temper tantrums!)

The importance of giving your chinchillas a strictly limited and appropriate diet cannot be overstated. It is critical that you stick to a simple and consistent diet when feeding your chinchillas: namely, quality chinchilla pellets; hay; grain supplement; fresh, clean water; and (optionally) the occasional chinchilla-approved treat—*and that is it!* No matter how much they beg or pester or how much you love feeding them, it is dangerous to both the short- and long-term health of your chinchillas to give them foods beyond the basic grains and hays. They are simply not equipped to digest such food. And don't give them salt licks; they get all the salt they need in their regular diet.

Chinchilla Pellets

The mainstay of the chinchilla diet is good-quality pellets made specifically for chinchillas. Pellets should *not* include animal fat, meat, bone meal, or fish products, as chinchillas are not meat eaters. Avoid any corn in the diet. Look for pellets that are at least 18 percent fiber, about 16 percent protein, and 2½ to 3 percent fat. Some good pellets, with their main ingredients listed, include:

- Oxbow Chinchilla Deluxe pellets (alfalfa meal, soybean hulls, wheat middlings, soybean meal) with 18–23 percent fiber, 16 percent protein, and 2½ percent fat
- Kaytee Timothy Complete Chinchilla Food (sun-cured timothy grass hay, dehydrated alfalfa meal, dehulled

soybean meal, wheat middlings, ground oats, ground wheat, oat hulls, dried beet pulp, dried cane molasses) with 22 percent fiber, 16 percent protein, and 2½ percent fat

- Blue Seal Hutch Extra 17 Growing/Pregnant Rabbit Pellets (alfalfa meal, wheat middlings, dehulled soybean meal, soybean hulls, wheat flour, oat mill by-product, heat processed soybeans, cane molasses) with 18 percent fiber, 17 percent protein, and 2½ percent fat
- Kline diet (alfalfa meal, wheat middlings, wheat bran, soybean oil meal, pulverized oats, cane molasses, linseed meal) with 20 percent fiber, 17 percent protein, and 3 percent fat
- Mazuri Chinchilla (alfalfa meal, dehulled soybean meal, ground soybean hulls, ground oats, wheat middlings, wheat germ, dried beet pulp, cane molasses) with 18 percent fiber, 20 percent protein, and 3 percent fat (if you use this feed, make sure to offset the high protein with plenty of timothy hay and a small amount of alfalfa hay)

Purchase chinchilla pellets that are fresh (check the milled date that tells when they were produced) and buy in small quantities: 5 pounds will last two chinchillas about two months. Pellets should retain their freshness for about three

Pellet Source

***If there is a grain store near you, you may be** able to purchase a 25-pound bag of just-milled pellets, which will be fresh, last long, and be surprisingly inexpensive. Bag up a few one-gallon Ziploc bags of the pellets, put the date on them, and store them in a cool, dark place. Use this supply for three months, then give away or discard any leftover pellets, or feed them to your woodland friends.*

months after the milled date and six months at most. Good pellets will have a noticeably pleasant, fresh smell when you open the bag; it reminds me a little bit of a just-mowed lawn. Old pellets smell like stale crackers, and chinchillas will turn up their noses rather than dig into these. Chinchillas will regulate the amount of pellets they eat (this is not the case with treats!), so always keep their food bowl filled with pellets. It is a good idea to give fresh pellets every day. Do not pour new pellets over the old, or those on the bottom will get stale. When the food gets low, dump the pellets out into the trash, wash the bowl, dry it well, and refill it.

One final note: if you ever change pellet brands, it must be done very gradually, over a period of several weeks. Start with 95 percent old pellets and mix in 5 percent of the new pellets; then, every few days, increase the proportion of new pellets to old, changing completely to the new brand after several weeks.

Hay

In addition to the pellets, feed a big handful of timothy hay every day—as much as your chins will consume; for variety, you can substitute alfalfa hay as a treat once a week. Chinchillas need high fiber (as much as 30 percent) in their total diet—much more than pellets provide—so hay is critical for making up the difference. Make sure to feed primarily the timothy hay, not alfalfa hay. Timothy hay is courser and better for grinding down the chinchillas' teeth. Alfalfa hay is too rich (high in protein) as a primary hay; moreover, because chinchillas think alfalfa hay is more yummy, they may get hooked on it and refuse the timothy hay in protest. Again, buy in small quantities, and keep the bag sealed and the hay dry.

Hay every day keeps the vet away. This chin helps herself to some timothy hay from a hanging hay feeder.

Supplement

Chinchillas also benefit from (and greatly enjoy) 1 teaspoon of supplement every day. A recipe for a homemade supplement is provided on page 100. Or you can order supplement from breeders who are already mixing large batches for their herds. (The breeder from whom you adopted your chinchillas may be willing to sell you supplement.) Commercially available supplement can be hard to find, but it is available online.

Giving food supplement every day, a teaspoon per chinchilla, will provide both health benefits and stimulation. Chinchillas clearly enjoy variety (chinchilla-approved only, please!) in their menu. Food supplement can be hand-fed as a bonding experience, served as a breakfast-time ritual, or given before feeding time in the evening. I guarantee it will be one of the day's highlights. Always feed supplement in an empty food bowl or separate treat bowl. It is not recommended that the supplement be sprinkled over a bowl full of pellets; in their zeal to

Kecia Santerre's Make-at-Home Supplement

***THE INGREDIENTS FOR THIS RECIPE CAN BE FOUND IN** health food stores and some grocery stores.*

1 cup old-fashioned oatmeal (the long-cooking kind, not quick or instant; also called rolled oats)

1 cup oat groats without hulls

1/2 cup barley without hulls

1/4 cup raw wheat germ

1/4 cup flax seed

1/4 cup red wheat bran

1 crushed multi-B vitamin pill

1 1/2 tablespoons cuttlebone (coarsely ground), from the bird section in a pet store

For a yummy twist, add bits of dehydrated rosehip, if available

A premixed enriched version of this supplement is available online at http://furryflowers.com. Supplement can be kept fresh in a sealed container for up to a month, and unused portions can be frozen for up to six months.

get at the tastier stuff, your chinchillas are likely to scatter the pellets and empty the bowl.

Treat Sparingly

In addition to providing the healthy and complete diet just described, many people want to give their chinchillas treats. As an alternative to giving store-bought treats, you can pick out the yummy stuff, such as the rolled oats, from the supplement and hand-feed these. These oats can also be used when taming and training your chinchillas.

Harmful Foods

***When it comes to feeding chinchillas, there are** more don'ts than dos. Rather than trying to remember everything not to feed a chinchilla, it is much easier to memorize the list of safe foods—pellets, hay, supplement—and strictly stick with the diet. Bottom line: do not experiment with any other foods.*

Type/Food to Avoid	Why It Is Harmful
Meat and dairy products	Chins are herbivores
Fresh or dried fruit, except for the occasional raisin or dried cranberry bit	Chins cannot digest much sugar
Vegetables	Can cause diarrhea
Peas, fresh corn, dried corn	May contain harmful toxins
Green grasses or green, leafy vegetables such as lettuce, broccoli, cabbage, spinach, and newly cut grasses	Can cause gas or bloat and are potentially fatal
Seeds or pits of fruit	Contain traces of arsenic, which can be fatal
Nuts and seeds (or other high-fat items)	High in fat and hard to digest; can cause liver disease
Dried coconut	Expands in the stomach with painful or deadly results
Chocolate	Can cause damage to both the digestive and nervous system
Processed "people food"	Will wreak havoc in the digestive tract

Giving chinchilla treats such as raisins is not necessary. Like giving cookies, cake and frosting, or candy to a child (and needless to say, never give these to a chinchilla!), giving sweet treats is not especially good for your chinchilla. Dried fruit has a high sugar content, and too much can be hard to digest and bad for the teeth. Nevertheless, because chinchillas crave treats so much, many owners cave in and do feed them goodies, and it cannot be denied that the occasional treat gives a chinchilla great pleasure. Whether you give treats is a personal choice. But once the habit is started, especially if treats are given at a predictable time of day, your chinchillas will come to expect it.

Two treats that chinchillas go bonkers over are raisins and Cheerios. The benefits of raisins are that they can help a constipated chinchilla become regular, and because they are a much-craved treat, raisins are useful in enticing a timid chinchilla out of the cage or convincing a rambunctious one to return. If you feed raisins, do so no more than a couple of times a week. Try cutting the raisin in quarters to prolong the enjoyment. Cheerios are a healthful alternative to raisins, and many chinchillas seem to love them just as much. One or two Cheerios can be fed a day.

The Daily Routine

Chinchillas are definitely nocturnal. They should have a quiet location to sleep in during the day and a ledge and nest box as sleeping spots. Mine alternate between the two, sometimes sleeping cuddled together in the nest box, and sometimes resting side by side on the ledge, with their heads drooping down and eyes glazed over or half closed. Like young children, chinchillas are adorable when they are sleeping. Sometimes they are so still that they look like the softest and cutest stuffed animals on earth.

A peaceful home allows this chinchilla to get a full day's rest.

Other times, you can tell they are real by their twitching whiskers as they dream. Chinchillas can fall asleep in the funniest of positions, such as leaning up against the food bowl on two paws, with eyes three-quarters closed, nodding off while nibbling on a midday snack!

Babies are less set in a nocturnal rhythm than are adults. They take many naps, day and night, with a period of awake time following naps, even in the daytime. Adults are more tired and cranky when awakened in the day, and they are resistant to invitations to wake up and play while the sun is shining.

Although you can't change your chinchillas from being nocturnal to diurnal, you can tweak their schedules somewhat and create more overlapping awake time between you and them by following a regular routine. A sample schedule could look like this: visit with your chinchillas for a while first thing in the morning, giving them fresh hay and a scratch under the chin, and then leave the house at 7 a.m., at which time the chinchillas go to bed. Come home from school at 3 p.m. (or from

Four friends enjoy chinchilla playtime.

work at 5 p.m.), and talk to and play with the chinchillas for thirty minutes. Giving the supplement at this time might help wake them up. Let them go back to sleep for a nap after that. If they ever seem tired or are having a "hard day on the shelf," skip the late-afternoon playtime and see if they are more receptive to coming out to play in the early evening. Give them a free-run time from 8 to 9 p.m. When they go back into their cage, have new pellets, fresh water, and more hay waiting for them. Before going to bed yourself, tune in to a radio station or switch on a television channel (an easy listening or family-oriented station at low volume is best for chinchillas).

Typically, chinchillas like vocal music. You may notice that your chins respond more positively to one type of music than to another. (In one herd, several chinchillas were seen dancing along to the Grateful Dead song *Sugar Magnolia*!) Turn off the TV or music in the morning.

It is important that chinchillas have a long quiet period in the day to sleep. Otherwise, they will become stressed and could get ill. A children's playroom with kids laughing and screaming and little fingers poking at the animals is not a good situation. The room doesn't have to be perfectly quiet, but the noise should be at a constant low level.

Grooming

Your chinchillas won't need much involvement on your part to maintain their thick, lustrous fur. Chinchillas take care of their own coats by grooming themselves and each other and by rolling in chinchilla dust. You need only provide the dust baths and give them an occasional combing to remove any dead hair or mats.

The Dust Bath

The most essential (and enjoyable) grooming activity for chinchillas is the dust bath. Take a bin or bowl (covered if possible) that is a little bigger than the chinchilla, and place in it a few tablespoons of chinchilla dust. Your chinchillas will roll and fluff in the stuff. I like to give the dust bath as part of their free-run time. If you do put the dust bath in the cage, do not leave it for more than a half hour, otherwise it becomes both a potty and a bath—not pretty!

In humid weather, fungus can be an issue. As a preventive measure in the humid months of the year, add 1 teaspoon of

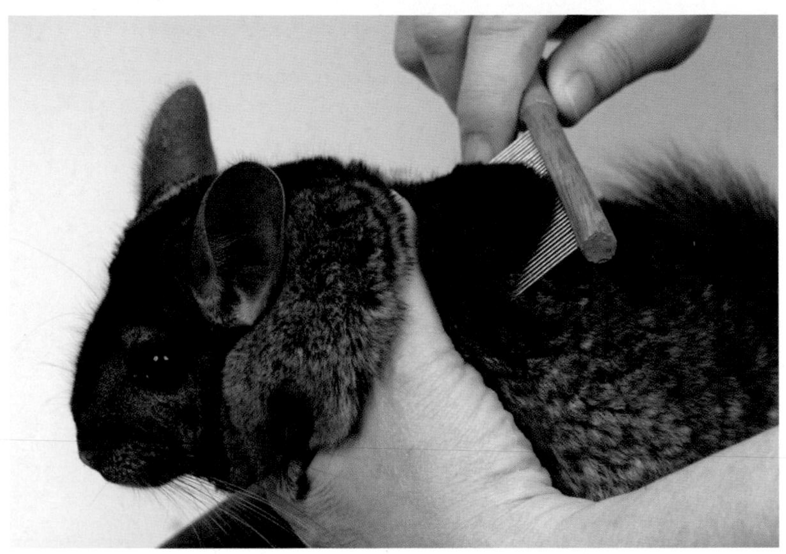

A pet owner combs out mats in a chinchilla's fur.

Desenex brand athlete's foot powder to 1 cup of chinchilla dust. Use 3 tablespoons of this mix for regular dust bathing. This is especially important if you don't have a dehumidifier (or air-conditioning, which in addition to blowing cool air, pulls moisture out of the air). Signs that your chinchilla has fungus are hair loss around the eyes, head, or nose, or bald spots with flaky, red skin. A few Desenex-laced dust baths should cure the problem.

Combing

Another grooming instrument is a special chinchilla comb (available online, for example, from http://www.chinchilla world.com). A wide-tooth flea comb also works. Use the comb to work out any mats in the fur. Chinchillas will develop mats if they get wet—for example, from a dripping water bottle or from urine. Never give your chinchillas a bath in water or get them wet (except in the case of a heatstroke emergency). They will

Care-at-a-Glance Checklist

NOTE: ALWAYS WASH YOUR HANDS BEFORE HANDLING CHINCHILLAS!

***CAGE:** House your chinchilla in a roomy galvanized steel cage with no ramps, no wire flooring, and no wooden parts, except for untreated, replaceable pine shelving.*

***WATER BOTTLE:** Use a hard plastic or glass water bottle mounted on the outside of the cage. It is very important to give fresh water every other day.*

***FOOD BOWL:** Use a 4-inch-diameter, tip-resistant, dome-shaped bowl or heavy crock-type bowl.*

***FOOD AND HAY:** Feed high-quality chinchilla pellets purchased fresh (check the milled date). Store food in a sealed container. Food should be checked and changed every day. Give a handful of timothy hay daily.*

***TREATS:** Give a supplement (see the recipe on page 100) or a half teaspoon of old-fashioned oatmeal, or rolled oats, every day. Limit raisins to a few times a week and no more than two a day.*

***HIDING AND CHEWING:** Provide a wooden house and a clean block of untreated pine to chew. Always supervise chinchillas when they run free, as they will chew electric cords and other hazardous materials.*

***DUST BATHING:** Never bathe chinchillas in water! Dust baths should be given a few times a week, or every day if you like, using about 3 tablespoons of dust per chinchilla.*

hate the experience, and their fur will become severely matted. Getting water on the fur can also cause skin fungus.

CHAPTER

6

Understanding and Training Your Chinchillas

Two chinchillas greet each other with a chinchilla kiss.

CHINCHILLAS LOVE TO EXPLORE AND PLAY, AND YES, THEY CAN be trained, too. The first step to training your chinchilla is to understand the nature of the beast. Chinchillas have poor vision, excellent hearing, and one of the more impressive communication repertoires in the animal kingdom. They are one of the few small animal species that can understand human speech, learn names (their own and their chin buddy's), pick up their favorite words, and be taught commands.

Chin-vision

Chinchillas are nearsighted, so objects at a distance are a blur. Quick motions seen at a distance are especially scary to prey animals (they wonder "What the heck is over there?" and "Are they after me?") and may send them scrambling for cover. Although chinchillas have pretty good night vision, it is hard for them to see in bright light. Try keeping the lights down low in the evening, and turn them off at night. If you are nearsighted yourself, interacting with them without your glasses on may make you appreciate more how they see the world. Many chinchillas like putting their faces close to yours to get a good look at you. But most do not like a mouth getting too near their necks, and they hate to be blown on (don't do this); it gives them a creepy feeling, as though they are about to get eaten.

Hearing

Chins have exceptional hearing and will know well in advance if you're coming near. If you follow a routine in feeding them, such as going to the cupboard to get the Cheerios and then walking upstairs with the cereal jiggling in the box, you will get a Pavlovian-like response. No drooling, but you can expect to see happy, excited chinchillas up at the front of the cage when you walk into their room. If your chins appear to randomly freak out, they probably heard a sound they associated with danger, maybe a door closing or a child outside playing—a sound that you couldn't hear.

Chinchillas like hearing different types of sounds. Many people have a TV in the chin room just for them. Chinchillas will appreciate it at night when they're up and you're not. Caretakers report that chins like the radio, too, especially singing (rather than instrumental music) and music that is melodic.

Chinchilla Communication

Chinchillas, with their strong verbal communication skills, have impressed and delighted scientists. Not only is their hearing acute,

He may not know how to spell, but it's likely that this chinchilla understands some human words when he hears them spoken.

they also have human speech recognition abilities that are very impressive for animals in their class. They can learn and respond to human words, but they can be a bit like cats in that they understand exactly what you're saying but choose to ignore you ("*Cage*? Yeah, right!"). When you speak to your chinchillas, have them learn a few short words that don't sound alike. You'll be surprised how quickly they learn and how much they can understand.

When talking to your chinchillas, get into the habit of saying the name of whichever one you're speaking to. Avoid using a variety of pet names for your chin at first. Chinchillas will learn their own names and the name of their cage mate. Calling your pets by name is a good way to get their attention. If you clap your hands or scold them with an "Awk!" they will stop what they're doing. Take it easy on such scolding, because if you do it too much, you may scare them. In addition to knowing their names, chins can be trained to respond to various words: *no*, *treat*, *play* (or *out*), *jump*, and *cage* (or *home*) are learned pretty quickly.

Chinchillas can master not only human speech but the languages of other animals as well. A couple of studies have even shown that chins will "speak squirrel" by imitating the sounds squirrels make. One pet chinchilla named Dusty is aware of the warning foot thumping and calls of the neighboring gerbils and degus, and Dusty briefly assesses the situation when any of them start to signal a warning. She is generally not impressed with what bothers them, but she definitely notices and checks.

Chin Chit-Chat

Chinchillas also have many forms of verbal communication. They are huge chatterboxes. Chinchillas are a bit like dogs in that they have several sounds they make that generally communicate pleasure or displeasure. Although this doesn't exactly qualify as language, if you watch and listen alternatively, you will find that your chin will tell you a lot. Check out http://www.chinchilla-sounds.de/index_en.htm if you want to hear a panoply of chin chatter.

Normal Barking: A chin's bark is a more guttural sound than a dog's bark is. It's a chin's attempt at being fierce. However, it can simply mean that the chin is not happy. Chinchillas also show off, barking simply because they can. Barking is their loudest sound, and some people believe it's a primary way of communicating danger to the rest of the herd.

Angry Bark: Sometimes, not all is well in Chinville. Chins bark to let each other know to cut it out. They can and do fight with each other, so listen for this type of sound, as it may be a precursor to their getting physical.

Whining: It can be hard to tell barking and whining apart. Whining is a lower-pitched call, resembling a seagull's, and it means "I want something"—a mate, food, or some necessity.

Squeaking: Usually, squeaking is done only by baby chins when they're hungry. I don't know if it's to attract the mom's attention or to annoy her to the point that she nurses the babies just to hush them up!

Whimpering: Whimpering can signal that chinchillas are somewhat disenchanted with what's going on. It doesn't necessarily mean they're in pain.

Crying: Crying usually means a chin is hurting. It can be painful to hear, because it is clearly the sound of an animal in misery. Because prey animals instinctively hide sickness or injury, by the time they admit to feeling pain, the pain has reached a severe threshold. Take this seriously; a trip to the veterinarian is probably in order.

Cooing (or Bleating): By cooing, your chins are telling you how much they approve of what you're doing and like the fact that you're their owner. They will also coo to each other.

Mating Sound: The female makes a special sound during mating season. The male responds by performing a ritual dance, wagging his tail. The best wagger gets the girl. If the male's dancing ability isn't up to par, the female, instead of making the mating sound, will gnash her teeth at him. And as males of any species know, that isn't a good sign!

Chirping: Chirping is good: this is a happy chin noise.

Chinchilla Body Language

Chins also communicate nonverbally and will let you know their needs as best they can through body language. Watching them

Grasping the proffered finger with tiny paws, this chinchilla grooms his favorite person. Being groomed by a chinchilla is an honor and a sign that you are one of the herd.

and seeing how they respond to you will be fascinating and will help you bond.

Here are some common chin nonverbal behaviors:

Begging: If they want something—usually food—they will do a pet poodle imitation: they'll sit up and beg! If this shameless attempt at cuteness works (and it probably will), you will find that this behavior increases in frequency.

Bouncing: If your chinnies have a big cage or run, they will literally bounce off the walls in their happiness to see you, especially when their normal feeding time or playtime draws near.

Dancing: Some chins have been known to dance; that is, they hop around on two feet in circles when they want something. It is just too cute, and if you encourage it, the chinchillas soon respond to what their adoring public wants.

Smiling: Chin owners can definitely tell when their pets are happy—the chins smile!

Winking: Winking is common and not a random behavior; it is meant to communicate. It says "Hey there!" "Aren't I cute?" "Pay attention to me!"—that sort of thing. If a chinchilla winks at you, wink back to return the greeting.

Blowing Their Fur: Fur slip occurs when a chinchilla that has been grabbed or is afraid suddenly lets loose a considerable portion of fur in an attempt to wriggle away. Chasing and grabbing a chinchilla, especially if done by a stranger, may trigger such a reaction. The more scared the chin is, the greater the amount of fur released. Don't repeat any action that gets your chinchilla upset enough to take his coat off! And don't panic—even though it may look as if a whole chinchilla is on your shirt, the actual chin will still look furry afterward, and the missing fur will grow back.

Stamping and Spitting: You may see stamping and spitting when, for example, a not completely tame chinchilla decides to lodge a protest against you and your bad ideas—such as extracting said chinchilla when wedged between two boxes on a high

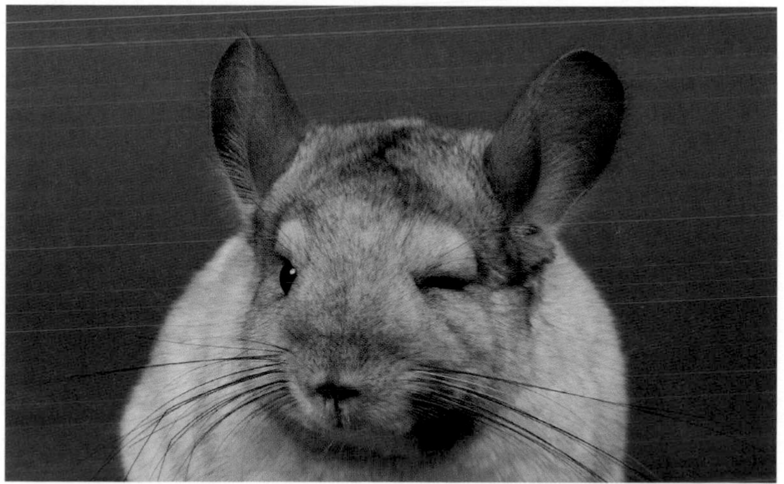

A chinchilla gives a cute wink. Winking is the animal's way of saying hello.

shelf and deep in a Chilean mountain crevice fantasy. Your chin may stomp a foot, lunge, and make a spitting sound at you. It sounds like "pffft!" Caution—this is chinchilla for "I've got *teeth*, and I'm not afraid to use 'em!"

Rearing Up on Hind Legs: Unlike begging, rearing up on the hind legs means the chin is trying to be fierce, not cute. The chinchilla will stand tall and tense, making eye contact. It is chinchilla for "Back off!" One false move, and a boy will chitter and bark, and a girl may shoot pee.

Rising Up on Hind Legs with Peeing: This is a chinchilla's final defense. It is usually done by a female and may be accompanied by barking. I'm not sure if it works in the wild unless the predator is very squeamish, but it tends to keep humans at bay.

Training: The First Steps

Training should occur only when you and the chinchilla are both in the mood and continue only as long as you are both having fun with it. Chinchillas must never be scolded during training; just ignore the incorrect behaviors and reward the correct (or close-to-correct) ones. Training begins by completely taming your chinchilla. (See chapter 4 for more on taming.) A chinchilla that is afraid cannot learn. If your chinchilla is timid or afraid around you, continue working on taming.

At the same time, teach your chinchilla that you are the dispenser of all things goodie. Every evening, when your chinchillas are just waking up and are both active and hungry, put a teaspoon of daily supplement in your hand, sit next to the cage, and hand-feed the oats and other grains in the supplement through the bars, all the while talking softly to your chinchillas.

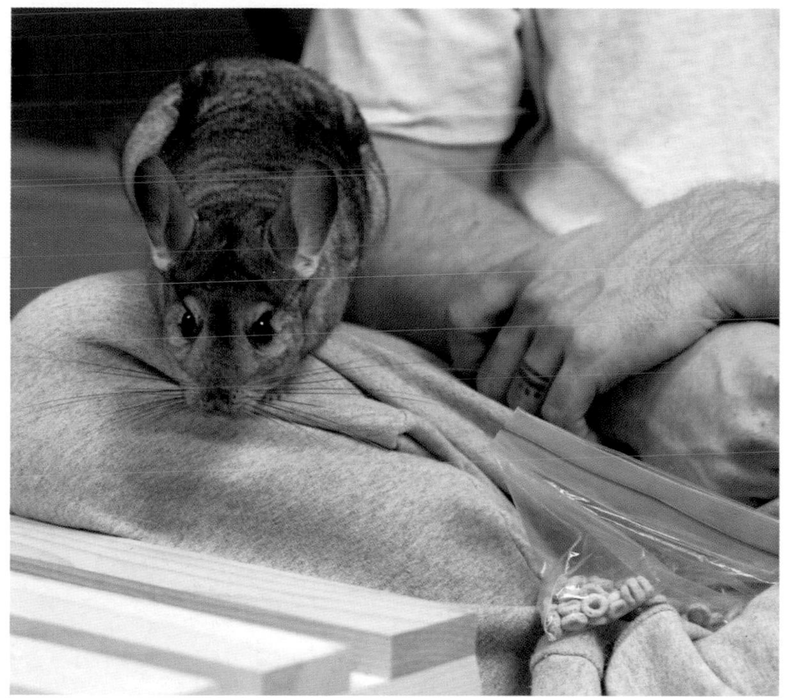

This chinchilla is learning how to sit with his owner, one of the first steps in the chin's training program.

The next step is to do this with the cage open, with your hand in the cage. And finally, have the chinchillas come out on your arms and sit in your lap while eating these treats.

Click Away

The next step in training is to associate the treat with a sound signal. You want to teach your chinchilla that a special sound equals food. Soon, hearing the sound will be just as rewarding as getting the food. And making the sound at the right time is much easier than delivering the treat. It is very important, though, that every time the sound is made, the treat is given afterward.

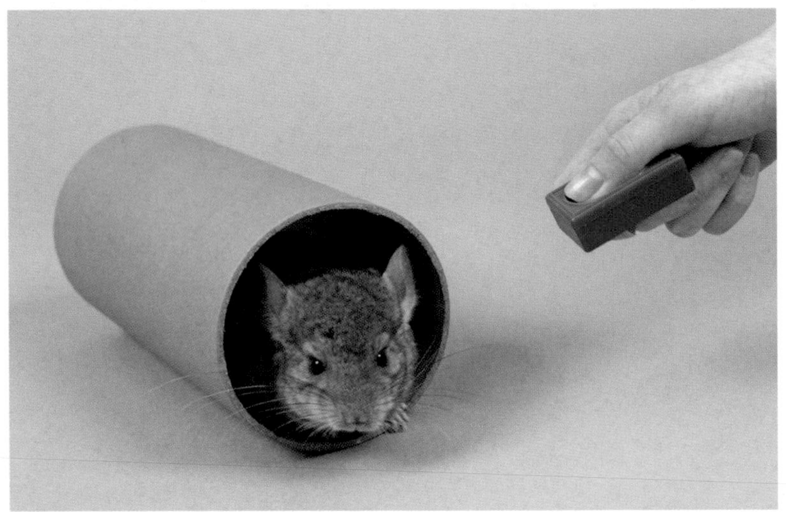

Click! A chinchilla owner uses the clicker, an excellent training tool, to reward her pet for running through a tube. Click at the moment your chin performs the desired trick.

The easiest way to do this is to use a clicker (which you can buy at any pet store). Get the quietest clicker you can find, or bend the metal piece to modify the one you buy to make the click barely audible. To teach your chinchilla to love the clicking sound, give a treat and click the clicker at the same time. Repeat the click-treat, click-treat pattern several times, and do this a few times each evening.

One of the potential problems with training an animal with food rewards is that you need to use a treat when behaviors you want (or an approximation of these) are displayed. Chinchillas can't have many treats. A treat such as a raisin is clearly out of the question (even cut in quarters, that is only four rewards every day or two). Instead, pick out the oats and other larger grains in the supplement, and use these as treats. You should be able to get a few dozen treats from the daily teaspoon of supplement.

Then, when the chinchillas have learned the significance of the click, you are ready to begin training. You can tell if they've learned it by giving a click and no treat; a chinchilla that knows the relation between the two will demand a treat, for example, by pushing at your hand.

Chinchilla-Inspired Tricks

Have you ever been to a dolphin or orca show at a marine park or city aquarium? You may see many of the standard tricks, such as waving a flipper, jumping up through a hoop, or leaping straight up and hitting a ball suspended at a great height. In addition to seeing these tricks, you may witness a complicated series of actions you've never seen before and wonder, how in the world did the trainer get that animal to do that trick?

Chances are that these elaborate tricks were developed cooperatively through a creative animal performing its own antics and an observant trainer shaping these into a repeatable sequence of events. I think this is the best and most enjoyable way to train a chinchilla. With the clicker in hand, wait until your chin does something very cute. Maybe, for example, your chinchilla likes to leap from the nest box to the top corner of the cage and just hang there. When the chin leaps, click. Orr and Lewin, in their book on clicker-training rabbits (see the Resources section), suggest that you imagine you are taking a picture of the trick, and click the clicker just when you would snap the camera shutter to capture a shot. Start the click when the animal is on the verge of performing it. After the click, give an oat treat. Your chinchilla is likely to hang there for a while, hoping for more snacks. If none come, the chin will leap down. At the next leap up, click and treat. Once your chin figures out that this action dispenses oats and repeats the action a

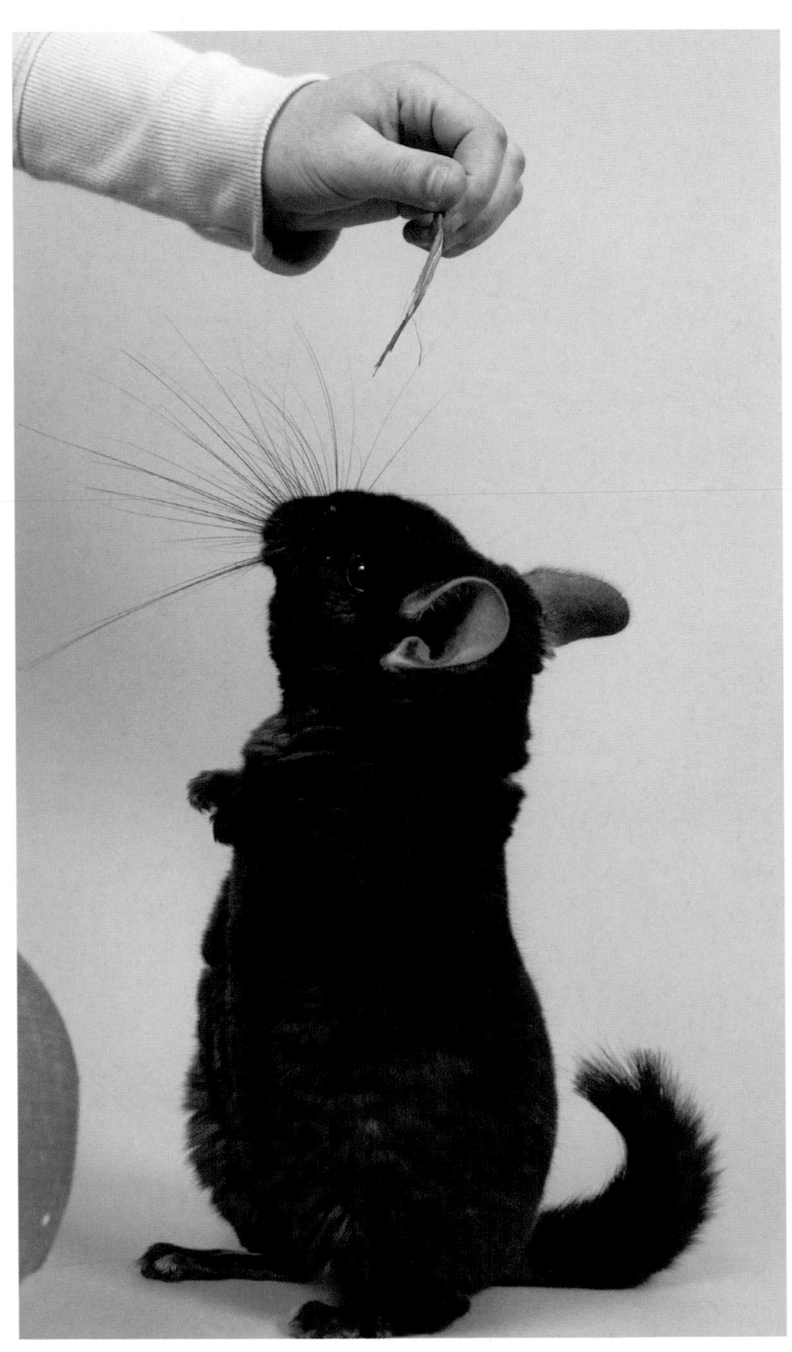

An Ebony chinchilla begs for a piece of hay.

few times in a row, introduce a command. Say "Boing" or whatever word you want to use (just use the same one each time), and maybe tap the corner or show the treat there as an added hint. Work on only one trick at a time until it is mastered.

Sometimes chinchillas will add variations to their tricks to get your attention, obtain more treats, or just show off. For example, yours might do a "double boing," leaping up the first time and just touching the corner and rapidly doing it again, the second time hanging there. You could click-reward the variation, making it the new definition of *boing*.

Once a chinchilla gets the idea of clicker training, your just sitting there with a clicker in one hand and treats in the other can produce some funny antics. When you see something you like, do a click-treat, and work on making that the next trick.

Trainer-Induced Tricks

The other way to train is the traditional one. In this case, you train the chin to perform a specific trick you are interested in teaching. Start with an easy trick that doesn't have many steps. This way, you and your chin will learn the concept of developing a trick though a series of successive approximations, or steps. A good one to start off with is running through a tube. Pick one about eight inches in diameter and a foot long. Watch your chin while he runs around the room. Find the path most frequently followed, and place the tube there. Now, wait for your chin to initiate these actions:

Step 1: Approaches the tube and sniffs or touches it: click-treat until your chin is spending a lot of time nosing the tube and pawing at it.

Step 2: Partially enters the tube: click-treat.

Step 3: Goes completely inside the tube: click-treat.

Step 4: Enters the tube and then emerges from the other side: click-treat.

Step 5: Runs through the tube when you introduce the command (for example, when you say "Tube"): click-treat.

If you and your chinchilla are enjoying these training sessions, try reading a whole book on the topic. There are books

To teach a chinchilla to perch on a shoulder, start with a chinchilla at shoulder level and some oats.

Give praise and an oat reward at each step of the trick.

This chinchilla has now learned to balance on his owner's shoulder.

available for teaching rabbits, birds, cats, and dogs with clickers, and the same techniques work with chinchillas. See the Resources section in this book for some suggestions. Good luck!

No Collars and Leashes!

A common question is whether a chinchilla can be taught to wear a collar or harness and be put on a leash. Collars, harnesses, and leashes are a big No for chinchillas. Chins have delicate bones and a tendency to bolt. This combination means that a collar and leash on a chinchilla are an emergency room accident (such as a broken neck) waiting to happen.

A better way to transport a chin is inside a small carrier or travel cage. Chinchillas should never be taken outdoors unless they are in a secure carrier. Chins are built for speed and distance, and if they escape outdoors, you will probably never see them again.

CHAPTER

7

Going On Vacation

A chinchilla shows an interest in a few oats. A treat such as oats can cheer up a lonely chin when her owner is away and her routine is disrupted.

BEFORE TRAVELING, YOU NEED TO DECIDE WHETHER TO LET YOUR chinchillas fend for themselves or have a pet sitter care for them while you are gone. In either case, there are many preparations you can make so that their separation from you and the change from their normal routine will be as smooth and stress free as possible. If you'll be gone for only a day or two, you could leave the chins home alone; beyond that, it is best that they be cared for either in your home or at the home of their sitter.

Home Alone

If the trip will be a short one, mount two 4-ounce water bottles on the outside of the cage a few days before you leave, and let the chins become accustomed to seeing and drinking from them. Fill

Before leaving these chinchillas home alone, their owner has fully stocked the cage with food, water, hay, and toys.

both water bottles the day before your trip; this way, you can ensure that they both dispense water and do not drip. With the water bottle backup, if one bottle runs dry, there will be a second source of water. Do *not* leave a carrot or other vegetable or fruit as a backup water source; the change in diet, as well as the large quantity of vegetable matter, is likely to cause diarrhea or a worse illness. Just before your departure, leave plenty of hay on the shelf or hay rack, and leave three times the normal amount of pellets.

If your chinchillas are used to having music playing at night, buy a socket timer (and test it to see that it works). These timers cost less than $10 and will turn the radio on and off at the normal times, so your chinchillas may barely know you're gone. Chinchilla breeders have found that a too-quiet environment will stress out a chinchilla as much as an overstimulating one will. It may upset your chinchillas if the normal household noises coming from other rooms are completely absent during the day. Consider leaving a television set playing (on a family channel) in a room down the hall. It should be barely audible in the day and be masked by the sound of the radio at night.

The biggest danger in leaving chinchillas alone is the possibility of a heat wave or of the air conditioner breaking down in warm weather. Consider moving the animals to the coolest part of the house so they can get used to it before you leave. One thing you don't want to do is make any big changes (such as moving the cage) right before your departure, as that will heap a double dose of stress on these little creatures that derive their comfort from routine. Give them a hand-fed supplement just before you go, tell them, "Chin up!" and reassure them that you won't be gone for long.

Hiring a Pet Sitter

If you're going to be away for more than a couple of days, it is probably best to have the chins take a road trip of their own to stay with a favorite aunt or family friend or, better yet, to have a pet sitter come to your place to care for them.

Take the time to find a neighbor or friend who can really bond with your chinchillas and provide emotional support when you are away. Chinchillas have definite opinions about people, and you may notice your chins immediately warm to certain people and are aloof with others. Make sure you compliment the people your chinnies choose as friends, and see if these people can be recruited as a support team during your absences. It's like cultivating a baby sitter for your children. If there is a friend or neighbor your chinchillas are particularly crazy about, try to get this person to care for them or have the person visit in addition to the regular pet sitter when you are away.

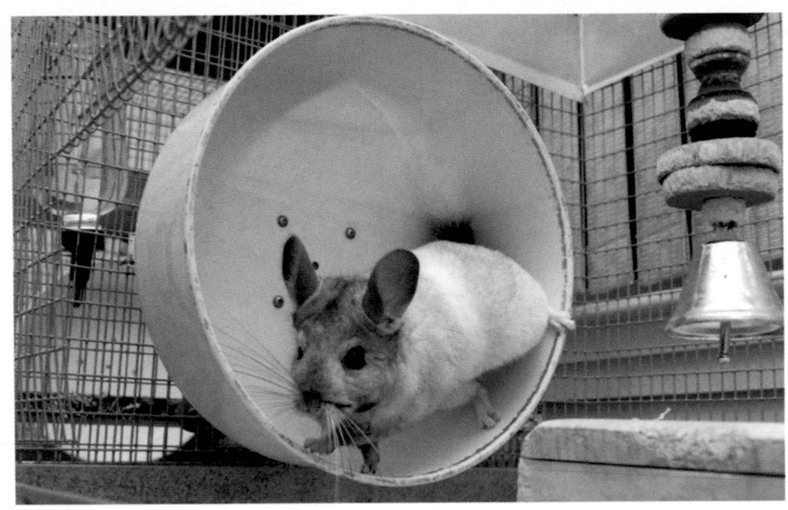

Despite being confined to a cage, this chinchilla is able to enjoy a good run using a wheel.

Making Preparations

When preparing for a long trip, put all the needed chinchilla supplies in one place for your pet sitter, as well as detailed written instructions and your phone number. Make sure you leave plenty of extra chinchilla food in case your trip gets delayed. Leave an extra water bottle, too, in case one breaks or malfunctions. Provide a checklist to let the pet sitter know what to do and expect. If you have several chinchillas, leave a picture of each chin, with the chin's name written on it, attached to the cage. A pet sitter should begin making visits before you leave so that the chin is not faced with meeting a stranger without you present; the new routine should already be established before you go.

One decision you have to make is how much freedom to allow your chins while you are gone: Should you let them roam free in one of the rooms? Should they even be allowed out of their cage? Chins jump much higher and move a lot faster than novices imagine they do, and since they are absolutely silent, they can be hard to find if they decide to play hide-and-seek with the pet sitter. A door ajar would be a porthole to freedom, and in no time at all, a clever chin would be impossible to find. If the chinchillas are out of their cage even for a bit, escape is a possibility. If you can't live with that happening, keep them caged until you come home.

If your chins are going to be staying in their cage for a while, make sure they have safe toys, such as hanging toys, wooden circles, and an exercise wheel or saucer. Again, introduce the wheel or saucer well in advance of your travels to make sure that they work properly and that the chinchillas know how to operate their home gym. Make sure the cage is spacious enough, with ledges for them to leap about on.

Whether the chins are to stay in their cage all of the time or enjoy occasional supervised free runs, you'll need a checklist of daily duties for the sitter. Here is a basic list:

- To check the temperature and humidity
- To make sure there is adequate food, hay, and water

A chinchilla chews an apple stick to help pass the time while her owner is away.

- To say hello to the chins and call them by name; sit next to the cage and talk to them for a while; and hand-feed some grains from the supplement

Have a list of contact information taped above the chinchilla cage so that you can be reached around the clock, in case of emergency. The list should include your cell phone number, hotel phone or host's house phone number, your veterinarian's number, the name and number of a supplier of the brand of food your chins eat, as well as any other important numbers. Ask the sitter to consult the veterinarian if the chinchillas are lethargic in the evening, have stopped eating and drinking, or seem to be in distress (see "Emergencies" for a handy list of guidelines).

Emergencies

In addition, let your sitter know of the potential chinchilla crises listed on page 131, and what to do for each.

When you return home, let the chinchillas out to play, especially if they've been in their cage for a while. If they seem to be giving you the cold shoulder, talk to them softly, and give them many hand-fed oats and even a raisin or two. They'll be in fine fettle in no time.

This chinchilla was lost in the house and then recovered in a live trap made for rabbits. If all else fails, this is a suitable way to bring your chin back to safety when she's gone on the lam.

Emergencies

Crisis	Action
The chin breaks free inside the house.	Use the tips listed in "Chinchilla on the Lam" (see chapter 4).
The chin gets outside the house.	Chances for recovery are slim, but try leaving the open cage outdoors near the exited door with a live animal trap baited with raisins next to the cage, and recruit all the neighbors in the search effort.
The chin is injured.	Call the veterinarian.
The chin won't eat or drink.	Call the veterinarian immediately.
The chin won't move.	Call the veterinarian immediately.
You run out of chinchilla food (or your Pug ate it).	Phone the food supplier (name and number are on the information sheet provided) and buy the same brand. Do not change the diet; chins can live on their hay and supplement for a day if need be.
The water bottle breaks.	Use the backup bottle, or buy another.
The chins are fighting.	Transfer one chin to the travel cage, with a water bottle and food.
The chin is making crying noises.	Call the owner and the veterinarian.
The chins throw a wild party.	No action needed. Owner will give chinnies a strict talking to upon return. Party on!

Traveling with Your Chinchillas

If you decide to take your chinchillas on vacation with you, it should be no problem at all. Many hotels, including most of the large chains, allow small pets for a modest fee (usually $15 to $25).

A great online resource for finding hotels is http://www.petswelcome.com. They can find and book a hotel for you and your pets. A number of hotel chains are franchised and have policies that apply locally. Many hotels, among them Days Inn, Comfort Inn, Econo Lodge, Marriott, Sheraton, Best Western, Hilton, and Four Seasons hotels across the country, allow chins. A few caveats apply when staying in a hotel with your pet:

- Most housekeeping staffs will not clean the room if the pet is left alone.
- All places require that the pet be in a carrier if taken outside the room. This is a very good idea for a chin, anyway, whether inside or outside the room. Some people do let their chinchillas stretch their legs in the bathroom. (Note, though, that not all hotel toilets have a toilet cover, which is a must for free-running chins.)
- Some hotel chains require that you be with your pet at all times.
- Get large amounts of newspaper for under and around the cage, and bring along your hand vacuum. You don't want to burden housekeeping with your chinchilla's amazing poop production!
- Leave a big tip, at least $5 a day.

Road Trip

Some chinchillas don't mind riding in the car; others don't like it much at all. Start off with short trips to see how yours react. When on the road, your pets can travel in their regular housing,

A travel cage, such as the one this chin is in, makes a safe and convenient temporary home.

provided there is room in the car and they are not bouncing off the walls of the cage. Otherwise, place them in a smaller travel cage. Covering either type of cage will help the chins feel more relaxed. Give them plenty of pellets and hay. Give a raisin before you go, to help avoid stress-induced constipation. Sometimes the water bottle will bang and drip. If so, you may want to remove it, but put it back on during stops and, of course, during overnight stays. Remove and replace any wet litter. While any animal will overheat if left in a closed car on a hot day, chinchillas are especially prone to heatstroke, so take them with you if you park the car in the heat, even for a few minutes.

Fur Can Fly!

Yes, you can take your chinchilla on the airplane. About 2 million pets a year cruise the friendly skies, and only in a handful of cases do the animals get lost, suffer an injury, or die. Since chinchillas do have stress issues, discuss with your veterinarian possible medication or other ways to minimize stress. Some veterinarians recommend giving any pet a small dose of tranquilizer before flying—find out what your veterinarian's feelings are on tranquilizing chins.

Most major airlines—among them, Alaska, American, Continental, Delta Air, Northwest, United, and US Airways—book pets on a first-come, first-served basis; have a carry-on limit of one kennel or one pet per person; require that the carrier fit under the seat; and limit the total number of checked kennels. Check the airline's policy—the company may require a veterinarian-signed bill of clean health and will have a list of requirements for approved travel cages. Policies also apply to the airlines' commuter partners. Southwest is the only major airline that does not fly pets at all.

As with ticket prices, pet passage costs vary among airlines and over time. As a rough estimate, a one-way carry-on is about $80; for animals checked as cargo, the cost is higher, starting at about $100. Some airlines accept pets only on flights within the United States. Others fly animals to destinations throughout North America as well as in Mexico, the Caribbean, and Bermuda. You can view an airline pet policies comparison at http://www.consumerreports.org/cro/travel/index.htm. Check with the individual airlines for details.

Your very best bet is to take your chins as a carry-on in a small container. Just add food, water, and either some litter or a not-so-messy grass mat, and your chins will be flying high. The alternative is to check them in as luggage; make sure that the airline knows they must be kept in a temperature-controlled environment.

If you're going to Hawaii and cannot leave the chinchillas at home, be aware that they will be quarantined for a few days upon arrival.

Hot Day in the City (or Country)

Chinnies are super critters, but their kryptonite is heat. When taking your chins on vacation, remember that heat kills chinchillas, and it is your job to make sure they don't die of heatstroke. Prolonged exposure to temperatures over 79 degrees Fahrenheit is dangerous, especially when combined with high humidity; an HH index (heat plus humidity reading) of 150 or more can be fatal. Don't take your chin outside in the heat of summer, especially in a parked car. Even a few minutes closed up in a hot car can be deadly.

CHAPTER

8

Health and Veterinary Care

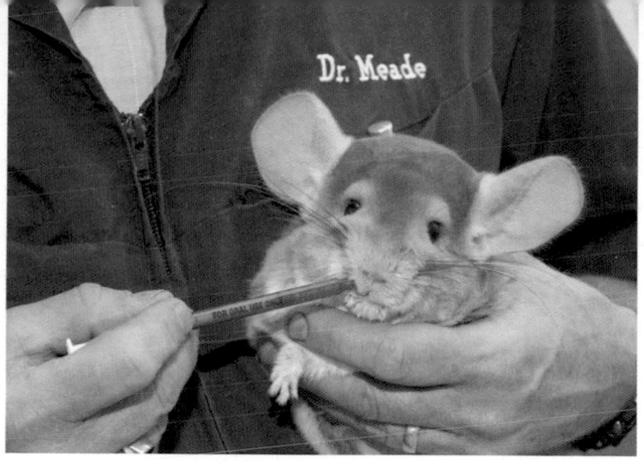

A veterinarian inserts oral medication behind this chinchilla's teeth.

CHINCHILLAS ARE VERY HARDY ANIMALS WITH FEW HEALTH issues when given the proper care. Many people report never having to bring their chinchillas to the veterinarian except for an initial checkup and routine well visits. Poor diet and improper husbandry, including not providing the hay and wood needed to keep the teeth in shape, are the most common reasons a chin develops problems. The good news is that ailments caused by improper diet and care are usually short lived and can heal on their own when the problem is fixed. The bad news is that a sick or stressed chinchilla can deteriorate quickly when health issues are not addressed.

I will go over common ailments that you can treat at home, as well as some emergencies and serious conditions that

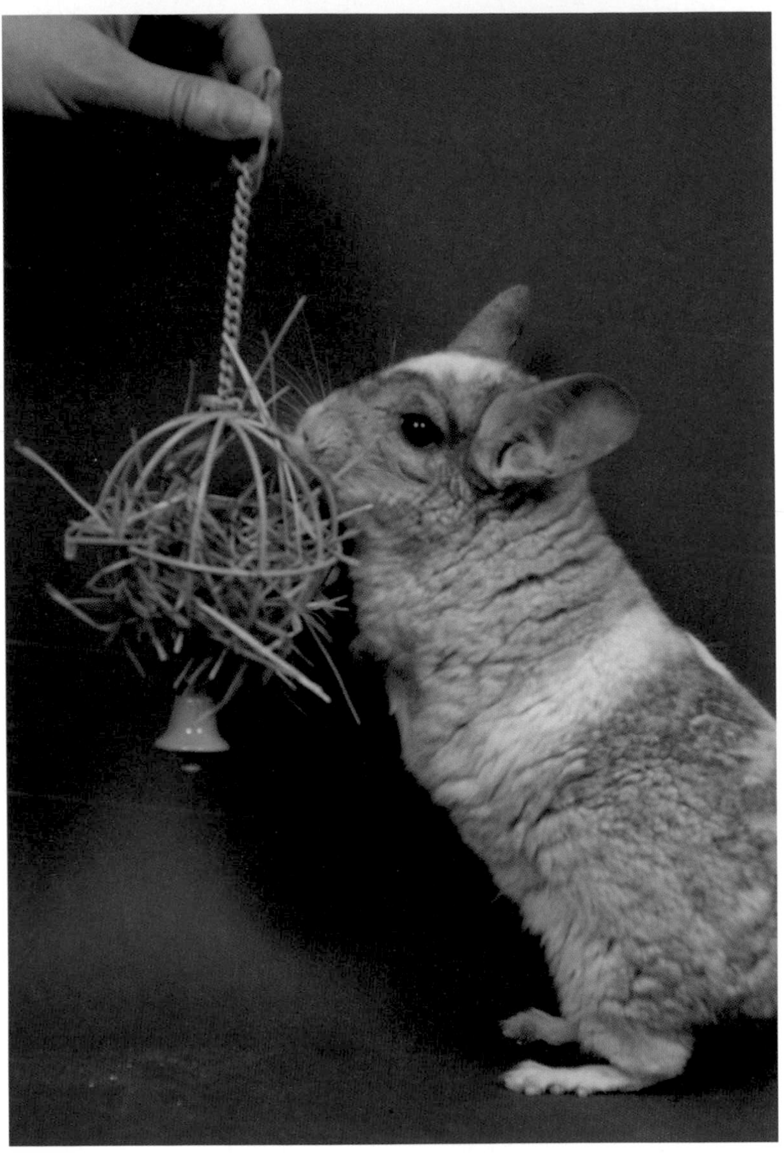

This chin enjoys his daily dose of hay, which helps grind his teeth down to the right length.

warrant a call to your veterinarian, and I'll help you know how to tell which is which. When in doubt, always pick up the phone and consult with your veterinarian.

Knowing When Your Chinchilla Is Sick

If you know your chins well, you'll notice when one of them starts to act in a strange way. Strange behavior may be a sign of illness. Being able to pick up on these subtle changes is one of the benefits of visiting and interacting with your chins often.

Be alert for the following signs in your chinchilla:

- Lack of usual response (such as coming for a daily treat)
- Dull or glossy eyes
- Unusual bowel activity (such as soft poops)
- Not eating or a change in eating or drinking habits
- Changes in mood
- Drooling, or constantly wet fur around the chin and mouth
- Bald spots, crusty parts of fur, or fur loss
- Light yellow or white teeth (babies are born with white teeth, but the adult's teeth should be a deep yellow to somewhat orange color)
- Seizures
- Changes in body weight (purchase a postal scale and weigh your chins on a weekly basis)
- Increase or decrease in urine production
- Blood in the urine
- Sneezing, coughing, or discharge from eyes or nose

If your chinchilla is sick, the veterinarian may prescribe medicines; be forewarned, though, that medicating a chinchilla is no easy feat! One idea for getting meds into a chinchilla while preserving the relationship you've worked so hard to build is to ask the veterinarian for a medicine that can be placed in the water bottle. Another idea is to give the chin a medicine-soaked raisin or Cheerio. While fully knowing that it is a poor-quality

This chinchilla is being weighed to make sure he is growing and maintaining a healthy weight. Weigh your chinchillas regularly, especially babies and seniors.

treat and giving you a suitably scornful look, your chin will probably not be able to resist the laced offering. If medication must be given orally, it may be wise to have another person play bad cop and carry out the treatment so that you can stay in the good cop (trust) relationship with your chinchilla. Veterinarians who treat small animals have access to medications in liquid form that are flavored as fruits, vegetables, and even alfalfa.

Common Emergencies

Even when a chinchilla is housed safely and is supervised when playing outside of the cage, accidents can happen. Serious conditions include a broken leg, choking, an eye injury, and a painful condition called hair rings, in which the hair wraps around the male genitals.

Broken Leg: A broken leg may not be obvious when a chinchilla is still; you may notice it during movement, though. A broken leg is an emergency that needs to be seen to immediately. Often, it is caused by poorly chosen housing that allows feet to get caught in wire ramps. As long as the fracture is new and not too severe, the veterinarian should be able to set a broken leg in a splint or cast or stabilize it with an internal pin. Your chinchilla may chew on the area or cast; a cone-shaped (Elizabethan) collar will prevent this. Chinchilla fractures heal quickly, with calluses forming in only a week or two, and the fracture itself healing in

This chinchilla's leg was broken on wire flooring, but the chin made a full recovery after having the leg set by a veterinarian.

three weeks. Rehab—that is, no leaping or free runs—takes several more weeks, however. Unfortunately, a serious fracture or one that goes unnoticed for a while may require amputation. The good news is that chinchillas can manage quite well on three legs.

Choking: Chinchillas can choke not only on a hazardous material such as gnawed plastic but also on food, bedding, and their own poop (which they nibble on for vitamins). You could either try to help them cough up the item or perform a chinnie Heimlich maneuver. Talk to your veterinarian in advance, during a well visit, about how to do this. If a healthy chinchilla dies suddenly, a necropsy may find choking to be the cause.

Eye Injuries: An eye injury is quite painful and requires immediate veterinarian attention. The injury often occurs when a chinchilla, for one reason or another, is bombing around the cage and scratches an eye on metal. The injured eye will take on a cloudy appearance. A veterinarian will give you two kinds of drops: one to dilate the pupil (which can dry the eye slightly), and one to treat the infection.

Hair Rings: Hair rings occur on male chinchillas when hair wraps around the penis; the result somewhat resembles a string of mini sausage links. The penis cannot retract, and the chinchilla becomes very unhappy and is unable to urinate. This is an emergency situation. Take the animal to your veterinarian immediately; after removal of the hair, fluid therapy, antibiotics, or other medical procedures may be necessary.

Nevertheless, chinchilla experts say the situation can be handled at home by massaging KY jelly or cooking oil into the area and detangling the hairs a few at a time. Or you could try slowly snipping away hairs with blunt-tipped scissors (made for baby fingernails or nose hairs).

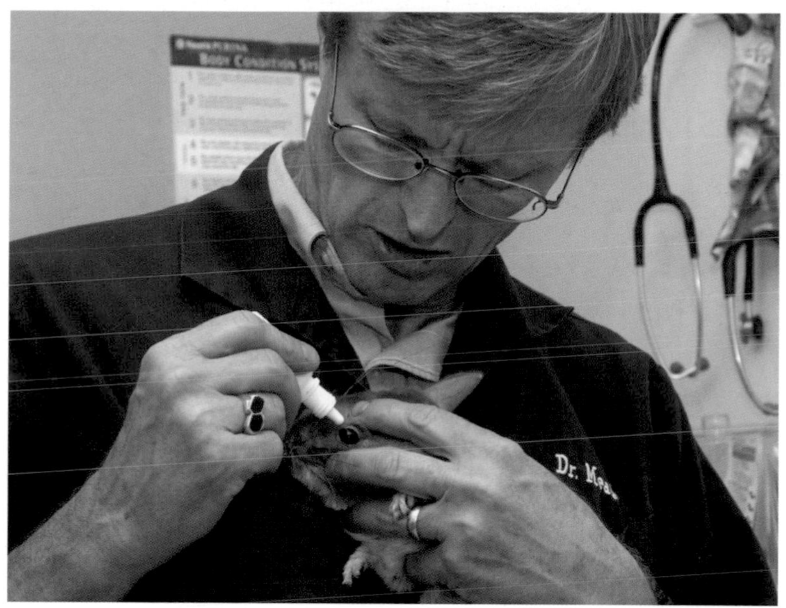

To administer eye medication to this chinchilla, the veterinarian holds the chin's eye open and inserts the drops, keeping the medication bottle a safe distance from the eye to avoid injury.

Chinchilla Ailments

Most chinchillas bred from healthy lines and given proper care will not suffer from any ailments. However, following are some health problems chinchillas could suffer from and suggestions for general first aid. Whenever possible, consult a veterinarian.

Constipation: Constipation can be caused by dehydration, too much protein, or stress. Stools will be hard and small. Try giving prune juice, a raisin, some yogurt (with active cultures), cat hairball medicine, or Metamucil. If there is no improvement or you hear the chinchilla whining or crying, consult a vet.

Cysts: A cyst is a soft tissue swelling caused by a fluid buildup under the skin. A veterinarian can drain a cyst, but if it recurs, it may need to be surgically removed.

Diarrhea: If diarrhea is short lived (lasting just a day), don't worry. If it goes on for much longer, then talk to your veterinarian, who can check for parasites under a microscope and look for indications of serious disease. Many times diarrhea is caused by feeding green food, changing the brand of food too quickly, or veering from the standard diet of hay, pellets, and water. Feeding only hay, without any treats or supplement, for a few days will usually do the trick. Put a little Pedialyte in your chin's water (this medication, used to hydrate human babies, does go bad, so replace the solution every few hours). Two other home remedies are to briefly switch from timothy hay to alfalfa and to give a small (one inch across) piece of unsweetened shredded wheat cereal.

Fungus (Ringworm): Warning! Chin fungus can and will spread to humans. Overcrowding, humidity, damp cages, damp hay, and the like encourage the growth of fungi. Make sure that the chin and the hay supply are dry and the humidity is low. One common chin fungus is ringworm, also known as athlete's foot. The signs are hair loss around the eyes, head, or nose or bald spots with flaky, red skin. Try mixing 1 teaspoon of Desenex brand anti-fungal powder (which contains the anti-fungal Miconazole) to 1 cup of chinchilla dust, and give your chinchillas a dust bath in about 3 teaspoons of this mix every day. If this doesn't do the trick, consult your veterinarian about how to treat the condition. Wear gloves when touching affected areas, so you don't get infected!

Fur Chewing: When chinchillas that are particularly sensitive to stress are kept in a stressful environment, they sometimes develop a habit of chewing on their fur. Stressors include boredom, overcrowding, a small cage, drafts, high temperature,

This chinchilla shows signs of fur chewing, a hereditary trait that can be aggravated by boredom and stress.

and an aggressive cage mate. Vitamin deficiency can play a part in the problem. The best way to stop fur chewing is to make the chinchilla's life less stressful through better housing and diet, more stimulation, gentle handling, and routine. For hardened fur chewers, anti-anxiety drugs may be prescribed by a veterinarian. Fur that is chewed needs to be plucked for it to regrow. Just don't stress out your chin even more by an inexpert plucking job! It may be best to have a veterinary technician do the plucking. Apply a soothing cream such as Dermisol, which your veterinarian can supply, to the bald areas. Fur chewing is a trait that can be passed down to offspring, so fur chewers should not be bred.

Gas or Bloat: Gas can be caused by feeding greens or fresh grasses, honey, or too much sugar: *a chinchilla must never eat these*. Gas is exceedingly painful for the chin, as this species cannot burp or pass gas to release the building pressure, the way people and some other animals can. Take away food for the day, and give your chinchilla plenty of exercise. A tiny nibble of baby aspirin might help ease the pain. If the pain continues for more than a day, consult your veterinarian. If the stomach appears distended or doughy, this is bloat, and you need to take your chinchilla to the veterinarian right away.

Heart Murmur: It is advisable to have a veterinarian check a newly purchased chinchilla or one that tires easily for a heart murmur. A heart murmur indicates a weakness in the heart valve or muscle. There are different grades and severities of heart murmur, and the heart can be strengthened with diet (for example, increased vitamin C) and the proper amount and type of exercise. Your veterinarian should be able to work with you on a treatment plan.

Heatstroke: Heatstroke occurs when the chinchilla gets overheated. You can prevent heatstroke by making sure that the temperature doesn't go higher than 79 degrees Fahrenheit and that the HH reading (heat plus humidity) is no more than 150.

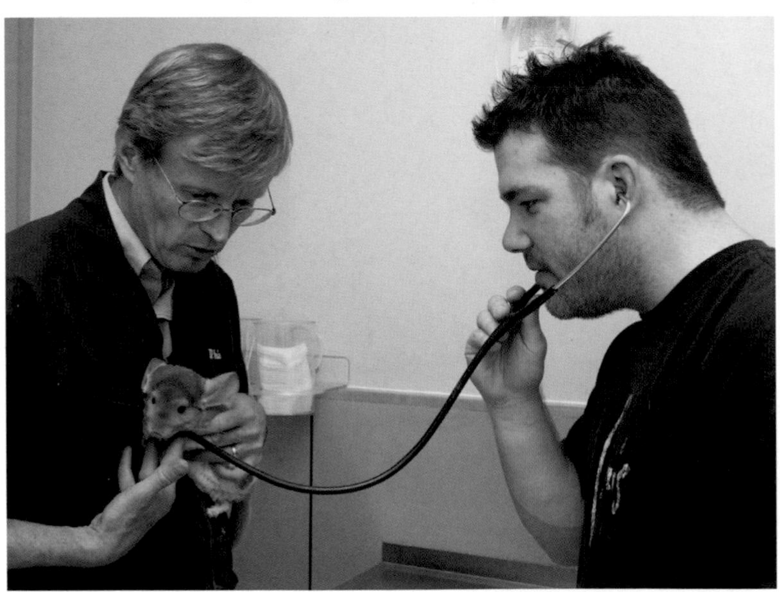

A pet owner listens to his chinchilla's heartbeat during a checkup.

Keep your chins cool with cool tiles, ice cubes, ice inside glass jars, air-conditioning, dehumidifiers, or whatever else works. If suffering from heatstroke, chinchillas will lie still, and their ears will be bright pink. They will pant and appear distressed, often lying on their sides. In rare cases, a chin will go into seizure and become unconscious; both conditions are emergencies that warrant seeking immediate veterinary care. If your chin gets too hot and you think you might lose your pet, immerse the animal up to the neck in tepid (lukewarm) to slightly cool (not cold!) water, if possible under the guidance of a veterinarian over the phone. Place the chinchilla in a cool, well-ventilated area. (This is the one and only situation in which a chinchilla should ever get wet.) Then take your chin to the veterinarian.

Malocclusion: This is a serious genetic defect that usually becomes obvious when a chinchilla is about eighteen months old. Either the front or back set of teeth are misaligned, such that no amount of gnawing will grind them down. The symptoms can be curbed for a while, sometimes for years, by the regular clipping and grinding down of the teeth by a veterinarian. Chinchillas with malocclusion need to gnaw wood and grind hay even more than other chins need to. They should never have soft foods or raisins, as these make them less hungry and less willing to eat the hard stuff their teeth need. The prognosis is best if the front, not the back, teeth are problematic. When the condition deteriorates to the point that chewing comfortably and eating properly are no longer possible, the animal should be euthanized. A chinchilla with malocclusion should never be bred, nor should the parents, as the condition will be passed to offspring.

Parasites: Because chinchillas have such thick hair (fifty to sixty hairs sprouting from each follicle), it is difficult for external parasites such as fleas and mites to get down to their skin. Internal parasites, however, can be a problem, depending on the water supply in the area. Check with your breeder to see if there are local problems with contaminated water; you may want to use bottled water. Boiling water for twenty minutes could be a cheaper alternative (let it cool before filling the water bottle). Giardia, as well as coccidia, cryptosporidia, tapeworms, hookworms, nematodes, roundworms, and pinworms can all find their way into the gastro-intestinal tract of a chin that ingests water or feces harboring these parasites. Giardia can be passed from chinchilla to chinchilla within a herd or at a show through contaminated feces, and it can be passed to people, too. Most internal parasites are treatable by a veterinarian; you may want to include a fresh stool sample (which your chin will be most cooperative about providing) during your chin's yearly well visit. In addition, bleach all metal cages and replace wooden shelves, wooden or cloth toys—anything nonmetal—to ensure that the chinchilla will not be reinfected. If internal parasites have been a problem before, consider using bottled or boiled water permanently.

Seizures: Seizures are most common in pregnant chins or chins that have just given birth, and they can be caused by calcium deficiency (a cuttlebone or a Tums can help prevent calcium deficiency). Seizures can also be caused by trauma, ingestion of toxins, tumors, liver disease, infection, and, in rare cases, diabetes. In any case, bring the chinchilla to the veterinarian.

Slobbers: Slobbers is the most common problem chins have. Their teeth, which are constantly growing, get overgrown, and that causes them to drool. An animal with slobbers will have wet fur around the mouth, which is unsightly and which they hate. Teeth that are overgrown have to be clipped by a veterinarian or veterinary technician. Prevention is easy, though: just see that you always have wood in some form or another (chew blocks, for example), timothy hay, and fresh water available.

If the chinchillas have plenty to gnaw and still get slobbers, it may indicate a broken tooth or the more serious malocclusion. The former requires feeding soft food, and the latter only hard food; both need veterinary attention.

White Teeth: White or light yellow teeth may be a sign of calcium deficiency—breeding females are especially susceptible. Offering a pregnant chinchilla a cuttlebone or a bit of a Tums every day can help correct this condition. White teeth in an adult chinchilla with a good diet are a cause for concern, and the animal should be seen by a veterinarian.

Wounds and Abscesses: If your chinchilla gets a minor scrape from a rough spot on the cage or during a fight, a mild antiseptic or saline solution can be applied to the wound. If it looks serious, contact your veterinarian. An abscess may need to be lanced and washed with diluted hydrogen peroxide; the veterinarian may prescribe an antibiotic.

Health and the Golden Years

When your chinchillas start to slow down, be aware of any age-related changes, and try to accommodate them. Weigh your chins every week, and consult a veterinarian if you see noticeable weight loss (or weight gain). If an older chin starts jumping less or misses a few times, move the ledges closer together or rearrange them into steps. Keep the litter deep to soften falls. Check for old-age-related conditions, such as cataracts, and if the chin's eyesight is failing, avoid rearranging the cage. Check the teeth often, and continue giving plenty of hay and wood to chew.

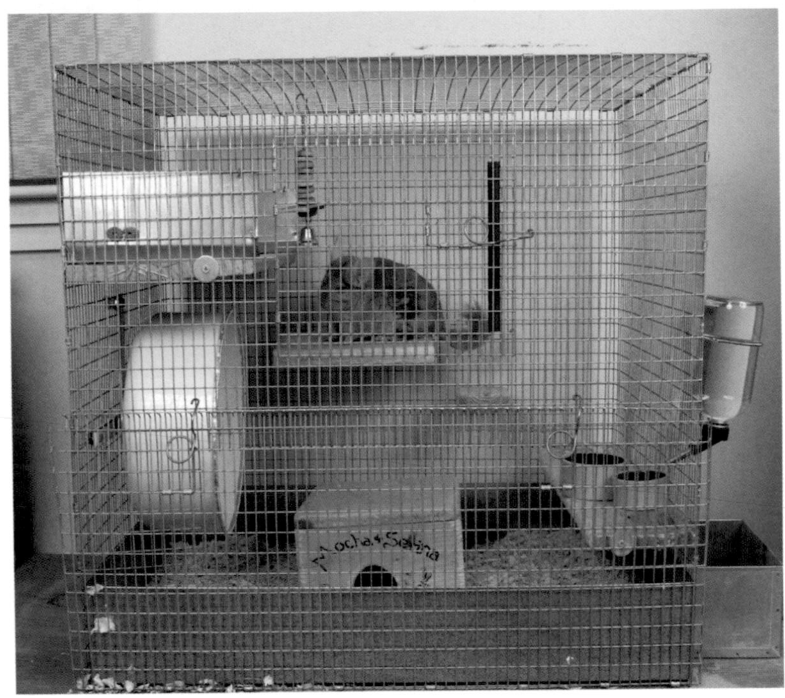

The ledges in this senior chinchilla's cage have been placed close together to facilitate leaping in his golden years.

And if you haven't already been doing so, take your seniors in to see a veterinarian for yearly well visits.

Holding On or Letting Go

One of the most difficult decisions a person can ever make is the decision to have a pet euthanized. It can feel as if you're playing God, making a choice that is heart wrenching and irreversible.

A comment a veterinarian will often hear is, "My chinchilla got very sick, very quickly. He was playing happily one day and went downhill the next." Not exactly. Prey animals are terrific actors. They instinctively know that predators look for the sick and aged to attack, so they will never show outward signs of sickness if they can help it. If they do, you can be sure they are very sick. A sick chin has to simultaneously battle an illness and put on a show.

Some signs that your chinchilla's quality of life is diminishing may include serious illness, the cumulative effects of old age, severely or completely restricted mobility, soft cries of pain, weight loss, and lack of interest in eating or drinking. Ask yourself whether your pet is able to enjoy normal chinnie activities. When a chin can't enjoy dust bathing, moving around, eating, and seeking affection, perhaps it is time for letting go. Immobility is particularly terrifying to prey animals; we humans can tolerate lying around in bed when we are ill, but a prey animal that cannot move lives in terror of becoming someone's dinner.

If you do decide on euthanasia, know that some veterinarians will perform this in the home, which would make the process easier on your chin. Remember, too, that the loss of one chinchilla will be a huge blow to the other. Chins are higher order, intelligent animals in many ways; to have a cage mate just up and disappear is stressful on them. It helps if you allow the remaining chin to see, sniff, and even touch the body and know the friend has died. Spend lots of time with the lone chin, giving several hours of exercise and out time every day. Some people provide a plush Cuddle Buddy (available at http://www.chinworld.com) for the chin to snuggle with during the mourning period (fibers could be ingested, though, so weigh the risks and benefits). The surviving chin may continue fine alone and even develop a stronger bond with you. If lonely and withdrawn for an extended period, however, the chin may benefit from and accept a new mate. A senior female and neutered male tend to get along well in such cases.

CHAPTER

9

Breeding and Raising Chinchillas

This baby chinchilla is on the move.

CHINCHILLAS HAVE ONE OF THE LONGEST GESTATION PERIODS OF any house pet, and the babies emerge fully furred and adorable. Tempting as it may be to breed your chinchillas, this is not a venture to be taken lightly. Bringing chinchilla babies into the world is a big responsibility because chins are highly intelligent and long-lived creatures. Before breeding them, make sure you either can keep the babies yourself or have loving, qualified homes lined up in advance. This chapter provides an overview of what is involved in breeding and raising chinchillas.

Breeding Chinchillas

Breeding chinchillas is not a simple matter and is best left to the experts. If you do want to breed these animals, the best approach is to become an expert. First read up on what is involved; there are lengthy Web sites and books dedicated to the topic. Read several to get a balanced picture. Then, work closely with a breeder—ideally the breeder from whom you adopted one or both of your chinchillas—and start slowly, with a single breeding pair. The breeder will know the chinchilla line and potential issues and will have an established relationship with a local veterinarian who knows these animals as well. The breeder may even be willing to come to your house to see your chinchilla (it can be difficult for a novice to tell if a mom-to-be is even pregnant until a baby begins to emerge). You may decide to give a baby from the first or a future litter to the breeder in exchange for these services.

The goal in breeding is to match two chinchillas that have excellent health, color, coats, conformation (body type and build), and temperament as well as complimentary genetic makeup. Such a match will produce babies that possess the same or even better qualities than those found in each parent. A pet,

This mom-to-be sleeps on her side, as is common toward the end of the four-month gestation period.

however beloved, that doesn't meet any one of these criteria is not suited for breeding.

Chinchillas shouldn't be bred until they are fully mature, that is, at least seven or eight months old. In some rodent species such as guinea pigs, females cannot be bred for the first time at an older age because by then, pelvic hardening, which leads to an inability to deliver babies, has set in. Pelvic hardening is not an issue with chinchillas; female chins can be bred at any age, and some continue to have a litter a year even when they are quite advanced in age.

Pregnancy

The female heat cycle is twenty-two to sixty days in length. Most pet chinchilla breeders breed chinchillas by housing a male and a female together. This way, the female will be bonded with the male and will allow him to mate with her when the time comes, and he won't miss his opportunity and have to wait a month or two for another chance. Male chinchillas are usually good dads, and some breeders let their males stay with the females and raise the litter. But often, a breeder will remove the male a few days before or right after the birth, for fear that the chinchilla dad, in his excitement to remate with the female, will stomp on the babies. Another reason many breeders remove the male is that they don't want to breed back, meaning allow the female to have back-to-back litters, which can deplete her energy and affect her health. Removing the male gives her a rest.

Females are pregnant for as long as 111 to 119 days (almost four months!), after which they will usually give birth to two or perhaps three babies. Pregnant and nursing chinchillas do not require much special care but do need extra protein and calcium.

Baby chinchillas, such as the two shown here, are born fully furred and surprisingly mobile.

Birth

Chinchillas are born fully furred, with eyes open, and are soon running about looking like teeny versions of their parents. They weigh 2 ounces or less at birth. The tail starts out wet and straight, dragging behind the newborn. When it curls up, that is the sign of a healthy baby. It is important that the breeding cage is safe for the newborns and that they can't slip through or get stuck in the wire (a 1 x ½ inch wire mesh works well). The biggest danger to newborns is hypothermia; make sure baby chins are kept warm at all times. Let the mommy chin heal for five days to a week before giving her a dust bath, and let her have a little private time during dust baths for the first couple of weeks. She will need to give her offspring some attention during their first attempts at dust bathing; little babies haven't quite mastered the combination of closing their eyes and rolling all at once!

A mother chinchilla nurses a baby. Baby chinchillas depend on their mother's milk for the first several weeks of life.

This baby cuddles with her mother for warmth and security.

Orphaned Babies

An orphaned baby chinchilla can be fostered by a female chinchilla that is either raising a new litter of kits or just weaning them. Even a momma guinea pig could be used as a foster mother. Because chinchillas are born so well developed, it is also possible to hand-raise orphaned babies, as a last resort; but the chins must be fed every two hours at first, day and night, if they are to survive. Prepare a formula of half evaporated milk (not condensed milk!) and half water, using water that has been boiled. You can add a drop of molasses or a tiny pinch of powdered glucose (from a drugstore). The formula should be warmed so that it matches the chin's internal temperature, which is about the same as a person's—97 to 100 degrees Fahrenheit. A drop of formula on your wrist should feel warm but not hot. Refrigerate the milk in a sealed plastic container to keep it fresh, and make up the formula right before feeding, throwing away any extra. After giving the formula, you'll have to massage the babies with a warm, moist cloth to stimulate the bathroom functions. Just remember that the most important thing is to keep the babies warm at all times.

Chinnie Childhood

At about two weeks of age, the babies discover mobility. They race, climb, and even start taking dust baths. It's a good idea to move the mom and her litter into a not-so-tall cage (about 16 inches) at or before this stage and to keep the bedding at the bottom deep in case the babies fall when climbing up the sides of the cage. Now, the kits start to nibble on food, but it is more for fun at this point, and they still must continue nursing for several more weeks.

A caregiver hand-feeds an orphan a special chinchilla formula.

Just ten days old, this baby chinchilla is already learning to climb.

These chinchillas copy many of their mother's behaviors, such as chewing on an apple stick.

From weeks two to eight, baby chinchillas are impossibly cute and irresistible. Fortunately, this is the perfect stage in their development for them to be handled every day and become very people oriented and friendly. Always wash your hands before touching them (keep some waterless antibacterial hand soap next to the cage), and make sure you are inside a penned-off or confined area. Sitting on the floor so they don't have far to fall, let them crawl on your hands and arms; when they get tired, let them take a nap in your lap. Don't keep them away from mom for too long, especially when they are nursing every few hours.

It is never too soon to start getting your young chins used to being handled for grooming and health checks. Practice running a comb softly through the fur, looking at the skin and fur, checking l checking the males for hair rings. If the chins are to :amine them the way a judge would. Encourage new ntinue this routine with the babies, too.

Chinchillas are fully weaned at about eight weeks. At this point, a professional breeder with multiple litters will transfer the babies to a nursery cage with other youngsters about the same age. A pet owner with one litter will move the youngsters into their own cage (unless they are to be paired permanently with a parent). A couple of weeks of living away from mom while still at the breeder's kennel helps the youngsters adjust to living on their own; the breeder will make sure during this time that the babies are eating and growing properly. This is a great time to put two

This adolescent chinchilla is cute but can be moody.

same-sex baby chinchillas together as cage mates. Chinchillas can go to a new home at between ten and twelve weeks of age.

Troublesome Teens

Chinchillas go through various growth stages, including a sometimes turbulent puberty. Female chinchillas are especially prone to growing pains. Your previously sweet and lovable little girl now grunts, spits, and may even shoot pee at you with dead-on aim. Rest assured that this phase, much like human adolescence, is only the hormones talking and will be short lived. Continue to spend time, even more time than you spent before, with your youths, showing them unconditional love and patience. Above all, don't lose your cool. Soon, they'll emerge as calm, confident, mature adult chins, more closely bonded with you than ever.

Coming Into Teeth

Chinchillas start chewing almost from birth, but chewing in earnest starts right around two years of age. You will notice at this time that the chinchilla you used to be able to let roam free for hours cannot be left alone for a second. Molding, table legs, boxes, and papers—nothing is safe from this suddenly ferocious gnawer! As this destructive drive increases, so does the chin's interest in toys, especially wooden ones. Make sure your two-year-old (and older) chinchillas always have plenty to chew inside the cage, such as a big block of wood, several small round wooden discs, or a hanging shish kebab of assorted wooden playthings.

All Grown Up and Places to Go

I've found that even though both of my chinchillas are well over two and all grown up now, our relationship continues to change

A chinchilla chews with gusto. At two years of age, a chinchilla starts to gnaw in earnest.

and grow. Lawrence, of late, has developed a desire to expand his horizons. He has taken particular interest in the door leading out of the room in which his cage is located and where he and Kera free run in the evening. Now, if I get up to leave for a minute, he races me to the door, allows himself to be scooped up, and wants to be taken around the house.

CHAPTER

10

Showing Chinchillas

A proud show chinchilla checks out his prize.

TODAY, THERE ARE TWO TYPES OF CHINCHILLA SHOWS: HOBBY shows and stock shows. Both use the same or similar standards. Stock shows are large, well-organized, regular events held primarily by and for ranchers who are looking for top quality and consistent fur in the herd. The majority of these shows exhibit live chinchillas, although some do include the judging of pelts (that is, furs). For the individual who is not averse to some exposure to the fur trade, it is an opportunity to see incredibly beautiful animals—the top chinchillas in the country. The second type of show is a hobby show for pet owners who seek to celebrate the chinchillas they love. Hobby shows can be hard to find and are sometimes held in conjunction with a 4-H event or as part of a larger small-animal show.

This chinchilla owner is equipped with a digital camera, a box, and some patience—all it takes to get a good entry for a virtual show.

Preparing for Virtual Shows

Some hobby shows are virtual shows, that is, pictures are judged online, so anyone, anywhere, can participate simply by e-mailing an electronic image taken with a digital camera or scanned from a photo.

Usually, in a virtual show, pictures are entered, but video shows are becoming more popular as show entries. Look at the photos from past winning entries, for example, at http://www.chinchillaclub.com/chinchillashow/, and see what works. Keep the following tips in mind:

Selection: Find your cutest chins. The nice thing is that if your best-looking chins are shy, they can still shine in a virtual show because entrants are judged only by their pictures.

Primp Your Chin: Give your chinchillas extra dust baths (one every day) in the weeks leading up to a day or two before the photo shoot. Do not use chinchilla dust right before the shoot, or the chin's color will look dull.

Groom the Fur: Comb your chin to make the fur look more even. Use a chinchilla grooming comb or a wide-tooth metal flea comb. In a pinch, you can use a men's hair comb. Make sure there are no knots or mats in the chinchilla's fur.

Go Digital: Digital cameras work best. Take tons of photos, and pick the very best ones. Use 3-megapixel resolution or higher, if possible. Digital video cameras work well, too, if you have software that can freeze a moment. Try constraining your chinchilla to a small area with a white background.

Attend to the Lighting: Lighting matters for people portraits; the same is true for chinnie portraits. Backlight, indirect light, and a flash that is separate from your camera will make a huge difference. Sunlight works well, too; take the picture indoors with your back to a window that lets in a lot of light.

Perspective: Take the photo at eye level or just higher. Read the show guidelines; usually, the judges want a front and a side view. Remember that your chinchillas may be more awake and up for a photo shoot first thing in the morning or late afternoon than they would be at midday.

These chinchillas have been carefully prepped months ahead of time for their big day at the show.

Preparing for Live Shows

The most obvious way in which a live show differs from a virtual show is that in a live show, chinchillas are handled and examined by a judge. Chinchillas that you intend to show should be held frequently from a young age by many different people so they become accustomed to strangers. In the weeks leading up to the show, practice the handling at home with a competent chinchilla person, having that person check your chinchilla as a judge would. Make sure the practice sessions go well so that your chinchilla knows what to expect and won't freak out when being judged at the show. Practice at the same time as the show so that the chin is comfortable being handled at that time of day: for example, practice in the late morning so the chinchilla gets used to being handled when sleepy.

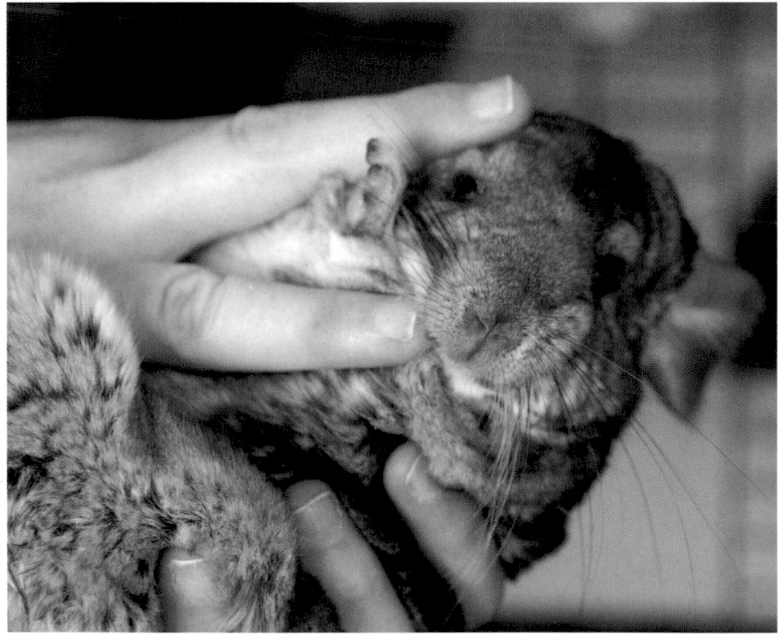

An owner handles her chinchilla. Handling a show chinchilla frequently and from an early age will help him be relaxed when examined by a judge.

While any pet deserves a high-quality diet, this is especially important for an animal that will be shown. In addition, prepare your chinchilla's coat (the same way you'd prepare it for a virtual show, with weekly combing and daily dust baths). But again, do not give a dust bath in the last two to three days before the show.

To get your chinchilla used to spending time in the show pen, start giving both dust baths and supplement inside the pen so the chin comes to like being in there. Note that for the day of the show, neither chinchilla dust nor supplies (such as toys or bowls) from the cage can be placed in the show cage, which needs to look clean and presentable. Car rides and crowds are other show conditions that you can get your chinchilla accustomed to ahead of time. Some exhibitors start with the smaller shows and work up to the larger ones, such as the nationals.

Show Standards

Most chinchilla shows, whether live or virtual, hobby or stock, use the same general standards. Some of the criteria used in judging are hard to describe. The best way to understand the standards is to first read them thoroughly and then get out to shows. Whether you are an exhibitor at a hobby show or a spectator at a stock show—both are valuable experiences—attending shows is the best antidote for what is called barn blindness (or maybe, for your own small in-home herd, a better term would be *bedroom blindness*!). Barn blindness is a condition in which you are so smitten with your own chinchillas (or their pedigrees) that you become blind to the fact that they are not top show-quality animals and are missing the mark in one or more areas.

It is difficult to visualize many of the standards from words alone; you will need to go to the shows and see how they apply to

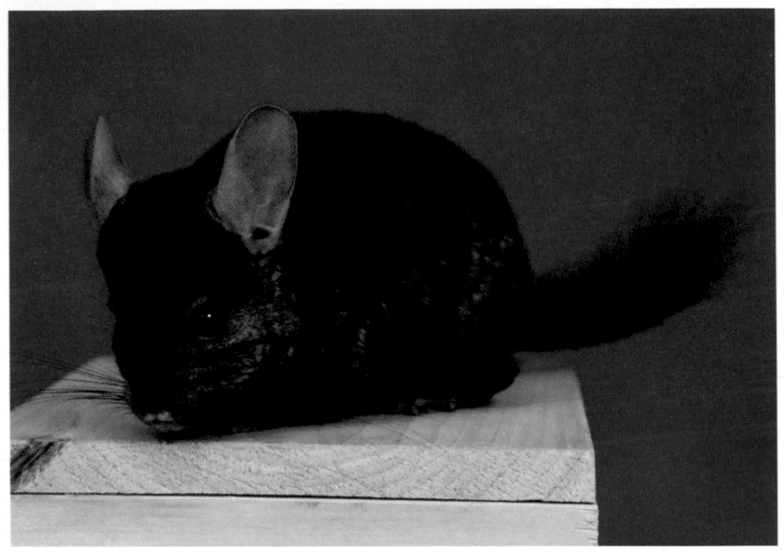

Here's a beautiful Ebony chinchilla, ready for his show debut.

appreciate their meaning. Nonetheless, to get you ready for your initial show experience, I'll make an attempt to explain the major categories in which your chin will be judged.

Fur Color: All chinchilla colors have their own standards. Whatever the color, it should appear clear, bright, and distinct. A color that is dull is a major fault, as is a hue that is vibrant but off color (having, for example, a nonstandard yellow or red tint). Often, the ideal chinchilla is said to be blue, which doesn't mean that the coat literally has a blue tint but rather that it shows no sign of any off color and thus achieves what is called clarity of color. Many chinchilla colors have veiling, or darkened fur tips. These should be carried throughout the coat, giving the chinchilla the appearance of being draped in a veil. Some chinchillas have a white belly. This should be a bright, stark white. Other chinchillas have coats that wrap, which means they have fur on the belly that matches the color of the fur on the back.

Fur Quality: The fur will be judged by its density (or thickness). Density is determined by the number of follicles and the number of hairs per follicle. Pet chinchillas usually have 50 to 60 hairs per follicle. Show chins may have more than 100 hairs per follicle (judges will not count hairs—they can tell by looking). Judges will also consider fur strength, or how resilient the fur is, which they call the snap. Guard hairs are longer, courser hairs (one per follicle) that contribute to fur strength. When a judge blows on the chinchilla, the fur should resist the pressure and stand up straight. (By the way, please refrain from blowing on exhibitors' chins to test the snap for yourself; this is bad form in chinchilla circles, as noted in the box entitled "Chinchilla Show Faux Pas.") Fur that lacks strength is said to be soft. Texture is the third part of fur quality. Silky is good. Woolly or cottony fur is not. The fur should give the appearance of being completely even (despite the fact that it must be of varying length—for example, longer at the neck—to achieve the right look). Fur must flow smoothly without swirls, waves, curls, rosettes, or any other observable patterns. Tails should be straight, not curled; a curled tail creates a part in the fur on the back.

Size and Conformation: In show chinchillas, a large chinchilla with a long, filled-out (but not fat) body is desirable. A winning show chinchilla is often said to be blocky or brick-shaped, which means that the animal has massive shoulders and a thick, short neck without a dip. The body should be more the large, chunky, compact *brevicaudata* body type described in chapter 1, as opposed to the leaner *lanigera* or smaller *costina* body types. Many pet chinchilla owners are surprised to see that winning show chinchillas are huge and may be twice the size of their pet chinchillas.

Chinchilla Show Faux Pas—Ten Mistakes to Avoid

1. ***Arriving at the show late***
2. ***Not helping out (chinchilla shows depend on volunteer power; look for opportunities to help)***
3. ***Stacking cages one on top of another (a chinchilla could get wet with water or pee)***
4. ***Leaving a mess of chinchilla fur, food, litter, and so on***
5. ***Grooming your chinchillas after others have started placing theirs on the judging table***
6. ***Smoking in the show room or near the animals***
7. ***Eating or drinking near the animals (spill on a would-be grand champion, and your name will be mud!)***
8. ***Blowing on someone else's chinchilla (leave snap testing to the judges) or otherwise stressing them***
9. ***Handling or approaching animals being judged, interfering with the judging, or criticizing the judges***
10. ***Having a side conversation when a judge is presenting (everyone in the show room should listen)***

Source: http://www.mutationchinchillas.com

Show Lingo: How to Talk the Talk

Chinchilla shows have their own special language. If you are able to talk the talk, you'll not only get much more out of the show, but you'll also impress the chinchilla show veterans by demonstrating that you've done your homework and are in the know.

On the one hand, if you hear terms such as *small for age*, *muddy*, and *soft*, you should not expect that chinchilla to go home with any ribbons. On the other hand, if you hear terms such as *extra large*, *shaped like a brick*, *stand up fur* (or *good snap*), and *clarity*, keep a close eye on that candidate. Maybe that chin

Chinchilla Show Terms

GOOD FUR COLOR

Blue—*fur that is clear and distinct in coloring, without any off-color tint*

Clear—*fur that is the right color*

Uniform—*fur that is evenly covered with veiling*

POOR FUR COLOR

No character—*fur that is not distinct and clear*

Off color—*a tint of brown, yellow, or red in the bar (the midshaft fur) or veiling (the tips)*

Washed out—*fur that looks dull because of poorly colored veiling or a muddy bar*

Shaded—*fur that is just a little bit on the dull side*

Muddy—*dull fur without luster or shine*

Mousy—*dull gray fur*

Casty—*fur that is off color, not clear*

Grotzen—*fur that is darker on the back of the head and down the back*

High on sides—*too much white on a white belly chinchilla*

Lacks finish—*color doesn't have that "wow" factor; it's not blue or it's not prime (prime means the coat is newly grown in)*

GOOD FUR DENSITY AND STRENGTH

Very dense (or close knit)—*follicles are close together, with many hairs growing from each*

Loft—*density plus fur strength (that is, resilience)*

Plushy—*it's all good: density, resilience, and fur length*

Snap—*coat shows good fur strength when the fur is blown, meaning the fur is resilient*

Stand up—*fur stands up straight*

POOR FUR DENSITY

Open (or open hips)—*fur lies open and does not stand up; especially apparent on the hips*

(cont.)

***Soft*—fur doesn't show good resilience when blown**
***Thin*—few strands of fur per follicle**
***Flat*—fur lies flat**
***Weak*—fur is too fine and is not resilient**
***Crew cut*—guard hairs are too short**
***Spiky*—guard hairs are too long (more than 1/16 inch longer than the fur)**
***Compact*—fur is dense, but too short (less than 1 1/8 inches)**

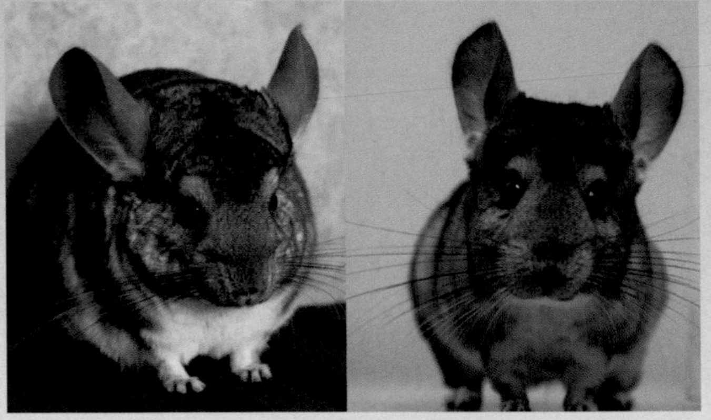

The chinchilla on the left is a show-quality chinchilla, big and blocky, with a magnificent coat. The chin on the right is pet quality.

GOOD FUR PATTERN

***Silky*—lustrous, smooth, even flow of fur that looks glossy; strands are neither too fine nor too course**
***Smooth*—no disturbances in the fur**
***Velvety*—uniform fur with the appearance of velvet**
***Even*—fur all appears to be of uniform length**
***Prime*—chinchilla has a thick, new coat of fur**

POOR FUR PATTERN

***New fur; unprimed; out of prime*—chinchilla has old fur; new coat is not completely grown in**

(cont.)

Past prime—fur has lost its luster; new fur will be coming in soon

Choppy; rippled; wavy; marcelled; swirly; cowlick—different types of patterns in fur that make it lack smoothness

Halo—lighter fur circling the back of the neck

Matted (or fur balls)—mats caused when new fur is entangled in dead fur that wasn't combed out

Cottony; woolly—fur is not smooth, but matted; woolly fur looks curly

Singed—fur tips appear burned; either it's old fur, or course dust was used for dust baths

Chewed—underfur is visible because the bar and veiling have been chewed

Not in show condition—a general remark to mean the chinchilla is not in prime, or is not smooth, or both

GOOD CONFORMATION

Large; extra large—a big animal that weighs more than 18 ounces, or even much bigger

Good size—large or extra large, big for the chin's age

Blocky—body is round, with wide shoulders and neck

Brevicaudata *type—large blocky body*

Full, short neck—contributes to the blocky appearance

POOR CONFORMATION

Narrow—thin shoulders and wide hips

Long—narrow body

Small for age—undersized adult

Dip in the neck—a dip that distracts from the desired blockiness

Medium full—slight dip in neck

Roached—fur is too high on neck and rises above head and shoulders

Bull neck—has a ruff of fur around the ears

Source: http://www.mutationchinchillas.com

This husky Beige male would be competitive at a chinchilla show.

will make it all the way to the show's grand champion. The boxes on pages 173–175 provide a list of show terms and definitions.

A Day at the Show

Before going to a show, carefully read all the guidelines on registration, show pen requirements, health inspection, and so on. Even if you are not showing this time, it will help you understand what is going on so you can ask intelligent questions of the exhibitors. One great way to learn is to volunteer ahead of time and see firsthand how shows are run. Plan to get to the show early so that you and any chinchillas you bring won't be rushed. Arriving early will also give you more time to meet and chat with other chinchilla fans and see top-winning chinchillas up close.

In a show at the national level, hundreds of chinchillas compete. Usually, these animals are the country's best and have spent the past several months competing in smaller shows. Taking part in the smaller shows cures ranchers of their barn blindness so they become expert at recognizing which of their chinchillas are of the best quality and will show best. It also prepares the chinchillas for a big show (what could be worse than nervous chinchillas that slip their fur while being judged?). Chinchillas from some of the top-winning lines will be up for adoption; a show could be a good place to acquire a chinchilla if you are interested in establishing your own show line. (See the section in chapter 4 on adjusting ranch chinchillas to home life, though, if you adopt one from a chinchilla rancher.)

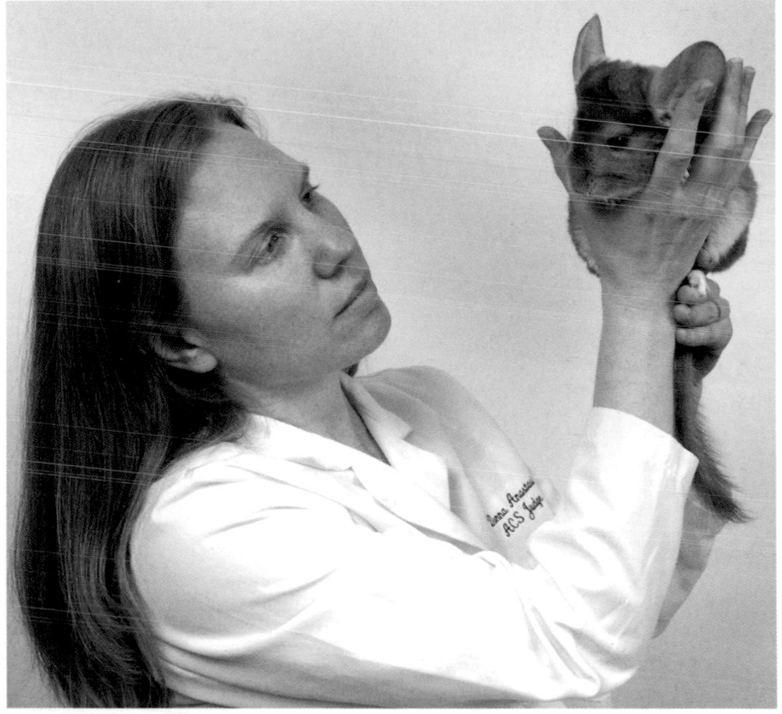

A judge checks for color, conformation, and fur quality.

A chinchilla show provides a wonderful opportunity to see various and unusual color mutations, such as this White chin.

The animals being exhibited will be registered the night before or the morning of the show. Each is identified by a ranch name and identification number located on an ear tag. This information is also marked on a card on the show cage, together with other information that judges need on color and section, gender, age (under or over seven months of age), and so forth. Then the exhibitors put their chinchillas in their individual show pens, with food and water.

Just before the judging begins, the chinchillas get a final combing (no dust bath, though, as it will dull the fur). They are separated and judged in several sections, each with subsections usually having to do with the darkness of the color (the White section is broken out differently). Categories are: Standard Gray (called Naturalle), Sapphire, Violet, Beige, Black, Charcoal/Ebony, and White. Color sections are broken down by phases, namely Light, Medium, Dark, and Extra Dark. Some colors can wrap, which means the belly fur matches the back fur, rather than being white. The white color section has a unique breakdown: White, White with Dark Guard Hair, Pink White, White Mosaic (patched), and Silver.

In the first round, the chinchillas are judged against the standard, not against each other. That means there can be several first place winners (or one or none at all). Then, all the blue ribbon winners compete to select best male, reserve male, best female, and reserve female in the section. The best chinchillas go on to the next level of competition. From these chinchillas, the champion male of show, reserve champion male, champion female of show, and reserve champion female are selected. From these final four, the runner-up is given the title Reserve Grand Show and the best of all is picked and named the Grand Show Champion.

There are other awards and honors presented to breeders for total points accumulated and average placing of chinchillas. There are special awards for junior breeders eighteen years and younger. Events and activities often are organized before, during, and after the main judging event. For example, there are always plenty of specialty supplies and chinchilla novelty items to buy. Often, a dinner or social gathering precedes or follows the judging and awards.

These chinchillas are playful and affectionate companions to the special person in their lives.

Chinchilla Shows of the Future

With the rising popularity of chinchillas as companion animals, I envision, in the next several years, the emergence of chinchilla fancier shows as a third major type of chinchilla show. A blending of stock and hobby shows, these fancier shows just might be the chinchilla shows of the future. Similar to AKC dog shows, fanciers will register their chinchillas (by name, not number), and individual animals in top conformation, color, and coat will compete for championship points over a series of shows or over the course of several years, under different judges. In addition to meeting all of the fur, size, and conformation standards, the contestants will have to be exceptional companion animals. They will be judged also on temperament and attitude; flashy, confident, friendly animals will show well and reap extra points to put them in the ribbons and win top honors. At least one budding organization I know of, the Chinchilla Fanciers of America, is working toward this goal.

Conclusion

Chinchillas are exotic and unique creatures with plenty to offer. Whether yours are grand champions or just plain old pets, they are beautiful animals and wonderful companions. Chinchillas are loyal friends with amazing memories. Each kindness bestowed is carefully stored away, and a fun moment is never forgotten. Enjoy many of both with your chinchillas for many years to come!

Resources

General Online Resources

http://www.chincare.com/
Packed with informative links and research

http://chinchillamagazine.com/pages/
Hundreds of articles from *The Chinchilla Community Magazine*. (You must be a member of the club; the cost is only $10 a year.)

http://smallanimalchannel.com
An online community with which to share your pictures, art, and essays about chinchillas and other critters; also offers magazines and other materials for purchase

Online Breeders and Rescue Organizations

http://www.chinchillaclub.com/breeder/
The Chinchilla Club breeder directory

http://www.etc-etc.com/yellowpg.htm
Chinchilla Yellow Pages

http://www.petfinder.com
Links to rescue chinchillas and rescue organizations

http://www.pets-on-the-net.com/directory/chinchilla/
Pets On The Net chinchilla breeders

Books

Moore, Arden. *Clicker Training: Simple Solutions*. BowTie Press, 2005.

Orr, J. and T. Lewin. *Getting Started Clicker Training with Your Rabbit*. Sunshine Books, 2006.

Richardson, Virginia. *Diseases of Small Domestic Rodents*. 2nd ed. Blackwell Publishing, 2003.

Vanderlip, Sharon L., DVM. *The Chinchilla Handbook*. Barron's Educational Series, 2006.

The two books below have useful information on chinchilla husbandry and history but may include too much information on the fur industry for many pet owners:

Kline, Alice. *After 40 Years Alice Kline Talks About Chinchillas*. Mutation Chinchilla Breeders' Association, 1995.

Ritchey, L., E. C. Cogswell, and R. Beeman. *The Joy of Chinchillas*. Private Printing, 2004.

Magazines

The Best of the Chinchilla Community Magazine. The Chinchilla Club, 2003.

Critters USA. BowTie Inc. magazine published annually.

Cages and Accessories

Custom Cage Works
http://www.cageworks.com/cage_gallery/ chin/index.html

Klubertanz Equipment Company
http://www.klubertanz.com/

Martin's Cages
http://www.martinscages.com/products/cages/chinchilla/

Quality Cage Company
http://www.qualitycage.com/chinchilla.html

Travel Cages, Nest Boxes Made with Wooden Dowels, and Supplement

http://furryflowers.com

Toys

http://www.chinworld.com
http://www.pet-chinchilla-toys.com

Clubs

Chinchilla Breeders Club
http://www.chinchillabreeders.org/

Pet Chinchilla Club
http://www.chinchillaclub.com

Forums

Forums provide a combination of facts and opinions; always research any advice before applying it, especially on the care and feeding of chinchillas. There are many chinchilla forums, including:

Chinchilla Club
http://www.chinchillaclub.com/forum/

Pets On The Net
http://www.pets-on-the-net.com/forums/

Chinchilla Sounds

http://www.chinchilla-sounds.de/index_en.htm
A fun site for you and your chinchillas to explore together, giving audio recordings of many sounds that chinchillas make

Glossary

back breeding: breeding back to back by leaving the male with a birthing female so that he will impregnate her again soon after the babies are delivered

bar: the midshaft section of the chinchilla's hair, between the roots of the hair and the tips

barn blindness: breeders' inability to see that their show animals are not quite up to standard; caused by spending too much time in their own "barns," examining the chinchillas and their pedigrees, when what's needed is to get out to a show

blue: the complete lack of any off-color tint in a chinchilla's fur, giving the color wonderful clarity and, on a dark gray or black chinchilla, the illusion of blue

Breeder Award: an award given to a breeder entering at least five chinchillas in a color section and achieving an average placing of third or higher

***brevicaudata*:** a species of chinchilla characterized by a large, blocky build, short tail, short ears, and flat nose

brevicaudata type: a term applied to any chinchilla that has *brevicaudata* characteristics, no matter what the species

clarity: perfect color: of the right hue, bright, and vibrant

coprophagy: a chinchilla's practice of eating its own feces for the vitamin B content and other nutrients; this is perfectly normal and healthy for a chinchilla

***costina*:** a type of *lanigera* chinchilla characterized by a small, lean build and short fur; prolific breeder inhabiting lower altitudes

Cuddle Buddy: a stuffed animal, made without eyes or other parts, for a lonely chinchilla to snuggle with

density: the thickness of a chinchilla's fur, determined by the number of follicles per inch of chinchilla and the number of hairs growing out of each follicle

dust bath: an essential aspect of chinchilla grooming; the animals roll and fluff in a fine dust powder called chinchilla dust to keep their fur clean and dry

euthanasia: putting an old or sick pet to sleep when it is in pain and can no longer enjoy even a minimal quality of life

fur slip: a chinchilla's sudden release of a portion of fur from the roots; chinchillas slip or "blow" their fur when frightened to surprise the predator and so loosen the predator's grip

gestation: the length of pregnancy, which is about four months for chinchillas

Grand Champion: the top-winning chinchilla in a national chinchilla show

guard hairs: course hairs (one per follicle) that grow just slightly longer than the other hairs in a chinchilla's coat and give the fur its strength and resilience

herd: a group of two or more chinchillas sharing the same mountainside territory, cage, or chinchilla room

heterozygous: having a dominant color gene that gives rise to the chinchilla's own fur color while at the same time carrying a recessive color gene that can be passed on to offspring to create recessive colors; abbreviated, in color variety names, to *hetero* + color (as in Hetero Ebony)

HHH (heat, haze, and humidity) or HH (heat and humidity) reading: a number that is the sum of the temperature in degrees Fahrenheit and the percentage of humidity; for a chinchilla's well-being, it should be well under 150 (an ideal temperature would be 50 to 75 degrees Fahrenheit, and humidity, 30 to 40 percent)

homozygous: carrying two like color genes, so if one homozygous chinchilla is bred to another of the same color, all babies will be the same color as the parents; abbreviated, in color variety names, to *homo* + color (such as Homo Beige) and indicates purebred

Hystricognathi: a suborder of the order Rodentia that includes chinchillas, guinea pigs, and porcupines but not rats, mice, hamsters, or gerbils

Junior Breeder Award: a certificate or trophy awarded to breeders eighteen years or under who have bred, raised, and prepared for show at least three winning chinchillas

***lanigera*:** a medium-size chinchilla species with long, thick fur and a long tail; domestic chinchillas are classified as *lanigera* chinchillas

ledges: untreated pine boards about an inch thick and a foot wide, cut to fit the cage and held in place with washers and heavy screws; they help make the most of the cage space (chinchillas need to jump from ledge to ledge for exercise)

malocclusion: a genetic condition in which the back or front teeth don't align and so cannot be ground down just by gnawing

Master Breeder Award: an award given to a breeder showing at least thirty chinchillas in at least three colors, with average placing of third or higher

mosaic: a fur pattern with patches of color instead of even coloring

mutation: a chinchilla color other than Standard Gray

Naturalle: a fancy term used at chinchilla shows for a Standard Gray (wild colored) chinchilla

nest box: a small box to sleep in during the day and to retreat to when scared or when needing to escape bright light (chinchillas are not nest builders, but they still need a nest box)

pellets: a chinchilla's main diet, consisting of alfalfa or timothy hay along with other ingredients, compressed into pellet form

pelvic hardening: a condition afflicting certain animal species; if females are not bred at a young age, the pelvis hardens and they are unable to deliver babies (this is not an issue with chinchillas)

phases: fur color classifications for chinchilla shows, such as Light, Medium, Dark, and Extra Dark

prime: a term describing a thick coat of hair that has newly grown in; all the old hair has grown out and been combed away

rancher: a person who breeds chinchillas for fur (typically, the chinchillas live in small cages and do not roam the ranch)

saucer: a wonderful running toy for a chinchilla that can be mounted inside the cage as an alternative to a wheel

slobbers: a condition in which a chinchilla's teeth become overgrown, causing the animal to drool

snap: the resiliency of the fur when it is blown on lightly; fur with no springiness to it stays flattened and open, whereas good fur snaps right back

supplement: a mixture of healthy grains, vitamins, and minerals specifically for chinchillas, to supplement their pellet and hay diet; the main ingredient is raw oats

Touch of Velvet (or Velvet): a variation that features darker fur on a face mask, along the back, and on paw bands; sometimes abbreviated TOV

underfur: the lowest portion of the hair, right next to the skin

veiling: the tips of the chinchilla's fur, so called because dark, uniform tips give the appearance of a veil, which is especially striking on a Black Velvet chinchilla

virtual show: a show held for fun, in which pictures or videos of chinchillas rather than the live chinchillas are judged

viscacha: a close wild relative of the chinchilla, also in the Chinchillidae family

weaned: having moved beyond the stage of nursing, which for chinchillas happens at around eight weeks of age, when their diet consists primarily of pellets and hay

well visit: a checkup at a veterinarian, scheduled for when the chinchilla first comes home and yearly thereafter; especially important for geriatric chins

woolly or cottony fur: fur that is matted rather than plush; can be due to lack of grooming or too much protein in the diet

wrap: back fur color that wraps around the whole chinchilla so the belly color matches the back, rather than being white

Index